A
ECT
ME
PET

"You see, Your Honor, I just beat a hare in a race . . . and I'd like to change my name to Flash!"

A PERFECT NAME FOR YOUR PET

by Texe and Wanda Marrs

illustrated by Paul Box

© 1983 by Wanda and Texe Marrs
Illustrations © 1983 by Paul Box

ISBN #0-89346-221-7

First Printing 1983

Heian International Inc.
P.O. Box 2402
South San Francisco, California 94080

Printed in the United States of America

Front cover photos © 1983 by Mitsuaki Iwago
Back cover photo © 1983 by Nobuo Honda

IN DEDICATION

Today there are more than 35 million pet dogs and 28 million pet cats in the United States. Over 7 million puppies and 5 million kittens are born annually to human "parents." In addition, millions of dogs and cats each year are adopted from humane society shelters and community dog pounds.

But canines and felines are not the only wonderful creatures who annually join American households. Countless millions of other pets, from gerbils to ferrets, enrich families with their personalities and presence.

Naturally, each of these pets needs a name to distinguish and establish its status as a member of the extended human family. After all, pets are just God's children with tails!

This book is dedicated to the millions of lucky Americans who become proud parents of one of these four-legged (or two-legged) children each year. As parents they have the enviable and gratifying task of giving their new pet a distinctive and lifelong calling card—a name. The over 3,500 pet names in this book will make this task both easy and fun.

A PERFECT NAME FOR YOUR PET

IN DEDICATION

NOTABLE QUOTE

"The naming of a kitten is the end proof of literary skill."

—Samuel Butler

INTRODUCTION

The practice of bestowing a proper and fitting name on a canine or feline is not new. Throughout recorded history, man has pondered what he should call his best friend. Kings, queens, and the royalty of Europe bequeathed special names on their pets, many of whom were accorded all the privileges (but few of the responsibilities) of court life. A pet without a name is not really a part of the family, but merely another animal. It is only when an animal or pet is named that he becomes a trusted and beloved member of the human family. A name provides personality and allows a pet to "fit in." It would be as unthinkable for a pet to remain unnamed as it would be for a human baby to go without a name.

A pet is always named by his human family. Names such as Rin Tin Tin, Lassie, Morris, Garfield, Miss Piggy, and Old Yeller bring signs of instant recognition when voiced aloud. It would be ludicrous to imagine any of these famous "personalities" being left nameless. After all, Lassie is not just *any* dog, nor is she just *any* collie dog. She is unique and one of a kind. And this is true of your own beloved family pet.

It does not matter whether your pet companion and family member is a dog, cat, rabbit, bird or, for that matter, an armadillo or pig. In this book, we will concentrate on the naming of cats and dogs. By so doing, we are not denying that people can be just as attached to other kinds of pets. But cats and dogs are the most popular of family pets, and we would be remiss if we did not devote as much attention as possible to their names.

You need not feel, however, if you own and love a mouse or a turtle that this book is not for you. The principles in this book and most of the names apply to any and all pets, regardless of breed or type.

There is no other pet like yours in the world. He or she is an individual. It is highly befitting then to give your pet a name to match its own singular personality and special physical attributes. That is what this book is all about.

Wanda and I are intimate observers of happenings in the world of pets and pet owners. We have been especially intrigued by the special bond that exists between a person and his or her pet. The loyalty between pet and owner is almost unique in the animal world. Only man has sought to domesticate other animals, and only man has made animals other than his own species beloved members of his family.

Only in such a "family" environment are the pet's unique characteristics and individual personality developed and molded. The name given a pet symbolizes his acceptance as an integral part of the family, and when used aloud, the name gives pleasure to the pet hearing it. Likewise, the human owner derives great satisfaction at seeing the pet respond to his or her name being called. The name, in effect, creates a lasting bond of friendship between the pet and the human. It helps to cement a lasting—and pleasing—relationship.

The naming of a pet is important, for it is in this way that the pet is initiated into a family. Once he begins to be called Rex, Kittie, Lassie, or Buffy, the pet ceases to be "just a dog or cat," or "just an animal." He becomes a bonafide member of the human family, with all the rights and privileges generally accorded such a status.

WHY A BOOK OF NAMES FOR PETS

There have been many books published on the topic of naming your baby (the human baby, that is), but few published on the naming of pets. This book is intended to fill that void. Naming a human baby is obviously of great importance, but naming a pet is also a significant milestone for a parent.

We often ask owners of a dog, cat, or other pet why they gave their pet its name and what factors they considered. Often, the answer is that the name just seemed to fit. But names for pets do not just mysteriously enter a person's consciousness. They are usually the result of an unconscious mental process and are based on a reservoir of the pet owner's life experiences. Sometimes, a suitable name "pops" into a person's mind almost immediately. Usually, however, the owner agonizes and frets over the naming of a pet, just as an expectant mother and father of a human baby do.

We hope this book will reduce some of the anguish of choosing a name by helping the new parent to make a proper "fit" or a name for a pet. It lists over four thousand possible names, from the ordinary "Rover" and "Tabby" to esoteric or unusual names that have special significance or meaning.

In addition, hundreds of names of heroic and famous pets and pets owned by famous people—presidents, movie stars, kings, authors, and other personalities—are listed. These exhaustive lists should make the task of selecting a name much easier and even fun.

Just as important, this book will assist the owner of a newly acquired pet to select a name that is both appropriate to the pet's personality and character and aesthetically pleasing to the human parents. Not only does it provide a large number of potential names, it also outlines a method of selection which will facilitate the selection of the "one" best name from among the thousands listed.

CONSIDERATIONS

Although our primary reason for writing this book is to help the pet owner who acquires a new pet, we hope to do more in this book than to just provide a list of pet name possibilities.

Too often, we hear critics accuse pet owners of excessive love and concern for animals. Such critics make fun of the care and attention pet lovers lavish on their pets. In this book, we hope to provide a basis for rejecting such criticism as being banal and nearsighted. It is our belief that the love and affection showered on domesticated pet animals by people is, in a world of human animosities, conflict, and contention, a shining example of the goodness that exists in the hearts of men and women. Thus, the respect for life demonstrated by pet owners and lovers is a precious commodity and not something to be carped about and criticized.

As for those who claim that the energies and money expended on pet care would be better spent on poor and needy examples of the human species, we can see no conflict between man and pet. Indeed, it has been our keen observation that the person who loves and respects animals is also likely to be one who has a similar healthy respect for the welfare of his fellow human beings.

Our purpose, then, is not only to assist the pet owner in naming his pet, but to affirm that the animal kingdom, and particularly those species which have endeared themselves as family pets, is worthy of human respect, attention, and utmost regard. Thus, on the following pages you will find, in addition to the valuable section on names, a discussion of the pet's place in our society as a legitimate member of the extended human family. This is no slighting of the human race, but an affirmation of man's humanitarian nature, need for companionship, and love of creation.

"Call me 'Superturtle' all you want, but you're not gonna get me to jump through that hoop!"

CHAPTER 1

THE NEW MEMBER OF THE FAMILY

THE NEW ARRIVAL

Nothing is more precious than to take a tiny puppy or kitten in one's arms and say silently, "This beautiful and cuddly creature is mine, to love, to cherish, and to enjoy." Few say these words or express these feelings openly, but deep inside they are there and every pet lover has felt them.

We have always loved to visit pet stores and animal shelters and observe the looks and gestures of those persons who have decided to take home a small bundle of fur. You can feel the excitement in the air, and the wondrous looks on their faces say much more than words ever could. And, it is not only the children that experience this sense of excitement and total joy. People of all ages, men and women, look to the ownership of a pet with happy anticipation. There is a strong bond of attachment which seems to exist between the new owner and the pet being adopted.

It is estimated that there are 130 million Americans who own pets. And the number of pets owned adds up to a whopping grand total of 610 million! That is almost three pets for every man, woman, and child in the United States! This incredible figure includes the total number of an assortment of pets, from turtles to fish, gerbils, mice—even toads and snakes.

By far, cats and dogs are the most popular of pets found in American homes. It does not, we believe, detract from the value and worth of other pets to say that there is something very special about dogs and cats. There is something special and endearing about every type of pet, no matter how ordinary or exotic.

PETS AS FAMILY

We have talked to scores of persons somehow involved in the pet world—workers at city dog pounds and humane shelters, persons who have lost or found a pet, veterinarians, breeders, pet shop owners, and many others. The one trait we find most common among true pet lovers is this: Fido, Rascal, Boomer, Fluffy, or Muffin are loved members of the family, just as are John, Larry, Mary, and the other "human" members of the family.

Indeed, some pet owners take offense at classifying their canine as a dog, or their feline as a cat. As one irate woman told us, "Don't call Pasha a dog. She's family!" Interestingly, this same woman went on to explain that she had acquired Pasha, a lovely poodle-terrier mix, from the "Adoption Agency" (translated—the local pound).

Most of us, of course, love and care for our pets while recognizing the fact that pets are *not* people. We see our dogs or cats as living and love-giving creatures that deserve respect in their own right, as an important part of the world in which we live and as a meaningful element in our own human lives. In this view, a dog or cat is to be loved, even cherished, not because it is a person but because . . . well, because it simply should be and by right, deserves to be.

Pets Have Come Up in the World

Several years ago, a book of names for pets would have been considered frivolous. No longer. Back in the '40s and '50s, when name books for human babies hit bestseller lists, some people also snickered.

"A name book for babies? How silly!" they scoffed. Yet, to expectant parents, a name book was not only proper, it symbolized all the pride and excitement they felt as they eagerly awaited the pitter-patter of little feet.

Today, prospective parents of a pet similarly look forward to a pitter-patter sound—that of tiny paws across their carpet or tile. Pets have indeed come up in the world!

Pets in Foreign Lands

It is quite indisputable that Americans consider their pawed and furried friends members of the family. But the notion of "pets as family" is a treasured tradition in other nations as well.

In Germany and France one frequently observes pet dogs in restaurants with their human family members. Invariably, the pet is well-behaved and almost never makes a fuss or causes problems for the manager of the dining establishment. This practice of taking the pet along for dinner is certainly not a hallowed American tradition!

To groom and prepare their dog to become a proper and respectable member of the family, many Europeans send their canine to a charm school or manners training seminar. *Time* magazine reported that the cost for a family to send their dog to one such school in Wagenfeld, West Germany, can run between $1100 and $1350. The school is called the Eton College for Dogs and run by a gentleman named Johannes Werner.

Werner supervises a faculty of 14 dog trainers who teach the pet how to conduct himself in public—in restaurants, hotels, on-ship, and even while the master is riding a horse. According to *Time,* at last count the Eton College for Dogs could boast over 10,000 impeccably mannered and polished graduates.

Evidently, the Japanese also treat their pets as near-people and as integral members of the family. This led to a humorous furor not long ago when an ad agency in Tokyo decided to use photogenic stray cats as models. Satoru Tsuda, manager of the ad agency, used the cats in a most unusual way. He dressed them up as people and photographed them in situations which poked fun at the modern Japanese lifestyle.

The clever Tsuda dressed the cats in black leather jackets and pictured them hotrodding on motorcycles. He also featured them as delinquent schoolgirls, members of an offbeat rock band, frazzled housewives, and intellectual school teachers.

The photographs were a sensation throughout Japan and were used on postcards, calendars, stationery, and a variety of other media. However, Tsuda's agency received a lot of flak from critics who stated he should be ashamed for his *humanizing* of cats! On the other hand, cat lovers protested that using cats as models, under such conditions as having to stand on their hind legs for the photographer, was *inhumane*! Tsuda defended his photos, explaining that the cats were made to stand on their hind legs only a few minutes at a time.

Man's loving instinct for pets and his desire to make his pets members of the family are so strong that even authoritarian communist regimes cannot extinguish it. In 1981, the Associated Press reported that communist government officials in Peking, China, had ordered all the residents of the city to destroy their pets. The reason given was an outbreak of rabies in the area.

Many city residents were too attached to their pets, however, to obey the government's instructions. One man, named Wang, was reported to have struck officials who came to his home to kill his dog. Another, named Chang, cursed the officials and warned, "If anyone touches the dog, I'll break his leg."

And Back in America

It seems that the love of pets and the large role they play in our lives are almost universal. Back home in the United States, it is also an historical fact.

About a century ago in Deadwood, South Dakota, a fellow named William Thompson noticed that the girls were awfully sad. They seemed to have a lot of lovers but no one to love. (There is a distinction, you know.)

Deadwood was a booming Western mining town in South Dakota. Thompson saw that the saloon ladies were visited by a motley crew of miners, down-and-out drifters, Indians, and soldiers. All of these characters gave the ladies their attention, but not their love.

So Thompson decided to make money out of this sorry situation. This astute and enterprising businessman, who owned a horse and wagon, made his way to nearby Cheyenne, Wyoming, a large city by Western standards back in the 1870s. There, he paid young children a quarter each for every cat they could catch and bring to his wagon. Soon the wagon was full of curious, meowing felines, and Thompson was on his way to Deadwood.

By the time he pulled up to the most popular saloon in town, the painted ladies of Deadwood had heard about his precious cargo, and they crowded around his wagon to see the cats. They screamed with delight when they spied the furry and energetic creatures and eagerly offered Thompson his asking price for the cats.

In less than an hour, all the cats were taken. Thompson contentedly counted his generous take. A profitable venture, he decided, as the count went past $1,000. The cat merchant, of course, was not the only satisfied person in Deadwood. His customers—the ladies of the saloons and dance halls—were thrilled beyond mention. They finally had someone to love and to truly return their love.

We could continue on and on about the wonderful way people adore and love the four-legged members of the human family. The point is this: people of all races, all religions, nationalities, and of every occupation and avocation instinctively love pets. The antics of Benji and the finicky act of Morris the Cat can be universally appreciated and understood.

WHY DO WE CHERISH PETS?

The dance hall ladies of 19th century Deadwood, South Dakota, provide the answer to the question, "Why do people cherish pets?" The reply, of course, is that they add companionship, roots, and stability. In other words, we cherish our pets because they are family.

The hunger of people for roots, stability, and companionship is such that they often grasp for weak, even inanimate substitutes. In Atlanta, Georgia, a firm is marketing life-size

dolls that come ready-made for a person or family thirsting for familial ties. The owner is given a "birth certificate" attesting that the doll is a "member" of his or her family.

In Philadelphia a great Teddy Bear Rally is held every year. At the inaugural rally last year, over 1,000 people brought their teddy bears to the city zoo, where the celebration honoring teddy bears was held. There were bears of all sizes, shapes, and colors, and their owners ranged from the youngest of children to Belle Louisa Brit, age 81, who displayed a teddy she got back in 1906 as a five-year-old.

Judges selected the best dressed bear, oldest bear, and the teddy that most resembled President Teddy Roosevelt. Sick bears were given medical attention at a teddy bear clinic.

The idea for the Teddy Bear Rally came from Great Britain where the first international Teddy Bear Rally was held in 1979 on the estate of the Marquess of Bath. The Marquess sent his representative, Clarence, to the Philadelphia affair. Clarence, a teddy bear (naturally), had his own seat on the airplane from London.

The Teddy Bear Rally provided clean, wholesome good times for the people who attended. It also illustrates the strong human need for permanent and reliable relationships.

Coincidentally, the teddy bear, which has been the stuffed animal favorite of generations of children, is named after President Theodore "Teddy" Roosevelt. President Roosevelt was an ardent hunter. However, his hunting for wild game was tempered by both his instincts for conservation of wild life and his love of nature, not to mention his enthusiasm for life. On one of his famous hunts in Colorado, the president came upon a baby bear. When he refused to shoot the cub, reporters christened it "Teddy Bear." This name soon caught on as a moniker for stuffed, toy bears. Soon teddy bears became the rage of the nation—and have been ever since.

The "pet rocks" fad several years ago can also perhaps be attributed to the modern-day need for stability and companionship. After all, a "pet rock" can certainly be trusted to remain with its owner and always be there.

11

THE VALUE OF PETS

Unlike a manufactured doll, teddy bear, or pet rock, a real, live dog, cat, or other pet can fill a void in the lives of modern-day Americans. This is why people have such a high regard for pets. This new attitude is now becoming so widespread and ingrained that pets have taken on a far deeper, more engrossing place in the lives of humans.

It seems only fair that pets today *should* be given a high place in human life. They deserve it! In the midst of an impersonal, automated, and computerized society, filled with impoverished and fleeting human relationships, comes the pet to the rescue with his boundless love and devotion for his owner.

What is so nice about pets is that they do not care what you look like, what color you are, how old you are, or how intelligent you might be. They love you regardless.

The story of Yuki, a yellow-brown mongrel dog owned by the late President Lyndon B. Johnson, illustrates this unique characteristic of pets. President Johnson adopted Yuki after his daughter, Luci, found the lovable dog abandoned at a gas station. Asked by reporters why he loved Yuki, an adopted mutt with no pedigree, the Texas president quipped, "Because he speaks with a Texas accent." Then, he added, "And because he loves me so much."

For children, psychologists say that loving pets is an important step toward learning to love other people. According to these experts, when children become responsible for the well-being of a pet and develop mutual love and affection, they learn to respect both themselves and other human beings.

Pets are even prescribed by many doctors and psychologists as therapy for people who have been hurt in human relationships. Pets are non-threatening. They help to draw the patient's feelings out, and they add a touch of care and humanity to the lives of the withdrawn patient.

Some theorists believe that a society that treats its pets well and sees to it that they are loved, not mistreated or abused, is also a society that respects the rights of people. In this connection it is ironic to note that the first documented child abuse conviction in America came about because of a law protecting animals.

Around the turn of the century in New York, a father was arrested for so severely beating his child, a three-year-old girl, that she required extended hospitalization. Unfortunately, there were no laws to prevent a man from assaulting a wife or his child. The family was considered the domain of the man, to do with as he pleased. However, the American Society for the Prevention of Cruelty to Animals (ASPCA) urged officials to proceed against the man by invoking a law on the books which forbade cruelty to animals. They did so and the man was convicted and imprisoned.

The case caused shock waves throughout the nation and resulted in every state eventually passing laws against abuse of children. Thus, it can be stated that animals have directly saved the lives and prevented the suffering of thousands of children ever since. This is just another reason why pets are valuable social resources.

However, the very best reason for owning a pet is because pets give people pleasure. It is just plain fun to own a pet. A dog or cat provides entertainment a person or family just cannot get from any other source.

Oftentimes, pet lovers are accused of foolishness and eccentricity. Naturally, this accusation is usually made by people who dislike pets. They cite outlandish examples to demonstrate their contention that pet lovers are foolish, overly sentimental, and even a little strange.

What these critics fail to realize is that pet lovers are folks with a keen sense of humor. Some pet owners do go a bit overboard on occasion, but then every group in society has its oddballs and characters. Many of the incidents or unusual or offbeat behavior by pet owners are carried out in the spirit of fun.

Just for the Fun of It

An example of the fun and spunky good times to be had from owning a pet was found by the authors recently in the classified ads section of a large city newspaper. In the Personals Department was this offbeat, but attention-getting item:

> *Energetic, 1½ year old puppy seeks intelligent woman to date 30 year old owner. Interests in travel, sports, and good food recommended. Good sense of humor and puppy treats required. Reply American-Statesman Box S-605.*

Then there is Mary Campanello of Hagerstown, Maryland. She had her German shepherd, Rex, ordained as a minister by the American Fellowship Church of Monterey, California. According to Ms. Campanello, as reported in the press, the Reverend Mr. Pooch "is authorized to perform all ministerial duties, including marriage ceremonies and religious services."

In Orlando Park, Illinois, an enterprising admirer of pets offers a wedding service for dogs, cats, and other pets. He charges $50 to conduct the wedding ceremony. This fee includes flowers and a three-layer wedding cake composed of hamburger, dog food, cat food, or bird seed. For an extra charge, this gentleman will dress the bride and groom in fetching little outfits.

Admittedly, this is a little unusual, to say the least. But it is also good fun, brings a chuckle to many lips, and smiles to a lot of faces.

There are many other examples of fun and humor on the part of pet owners and lovers. For instance, a California company put a new dog food on the market which appeals to survivalists—people who are worried about holing up in some mountain retreat during a nuclear war, the chaos of a depression, or other disaster. The can's label has a picture of a dog with a medieval helmet on his head. The name of the dog food—"Sir Vival."

In Dover, Ohio, last year, Shelly Cook did not like it when her husband, Jim, demanded she get rid of the ten puppies to which her female golden retriever had just given birth.

"They're just so cute and lovable," she pleaded.

"It's either the dogs or me," retorted Jim.

After considerable thought, Mrs. Cook finally decided to publish the following classified ad in the local Philadelphia newspaper:

Husband says either he or puppies must go. Puppies are half golden retrievers, playful, cute. Husband is cross and unsympathetic. Your choice free.

According to press reports, Mrs. Cook received many inquiries about the ad. Several women callers wanted to know what her husband looked like and how much money he made, but none offered to take him off her hands. As far as the puppies were concerned, however, the ad was a resounding success. All ten went quickly.

Mrs. Cook said her husband laughed and took it all good-naturedly, although he was a little surprised all the women chose the puppies over him.

There are many other tales of humorous and zany behavior on the part of pet people. An organization in California, Single Animal Lovers, was formed specializing in matching up singles who respect and cherish pets. According to Linda Wexler, founder of the group, their favorite story is that of the pairing of two goldfish lovers. On their first date they took their pet goldfish on a tour of Marine World.

As we mentioned, stories like these inspire those who detest pets to ridicule and accuse pet lovers of silliness. But a look at society itself quickly dispels this notion. The craziness of war, the specter of people fighting over religion, the soaring crime rate, corruption in business and government, and a hundred other social and political ills and problems attest to the fact that there are a lot of nutty and even perverse people in our world. It is difficult, then, to point a finger at harmless lovers of pets.

In fact, the wackiness of a minority of pet lovers is perhaps a cause for celebration. What better way for people to let off steam and frustration than to pamper a pet? Or to generate laughter and good times from pet behavior? And who can be so petty and churlish as to deny that people get great pleasure from their pets.

For instance, take the example of the late President Franklin D. Roosevelt. FDR often claimed that his very best friend was his loyal dog Fala. A scrappy and playful black Scotch terrier, Fala was with Roosevelt at every important World War I conference. Fala was introduced to every dignitary that visited the White House and he sat contentedly at the president's feet during cabinet meetings. The love of his dog sustained Roosevelt during the hardships of economic depression and war.

Franklin Roosevelt was not the only president who could be accused of an overabundance of love for pets (if there is such a thing as *over*abundance). History is packed with touching—and often humorous—tales of White House residents whose exploits illustrate how crazy they were about pets.

There is former President Lyndon B. Johnson, for example, mentioned earlier in the story of Yuki, the adopted stray mutt.

"Dogs," the late president once told an interviewer as he sat on the porch of his Johnson City ranch home, "have always been my friends." To prove his point, Johnson proceeded to sing a duet with one of his dogs—to the consternation and delight of the interviewer.

Calvin Coolidge is another who derived untold pleasure from his pets. When Coolidge was president, the First Family kept a large number of pets at the White House. The list included cats, dogs, a swan, and racoons. One of the president's favorites was Rob Roy, a collie.

The president treated Rob Roy as he would have treated a close human friend. The two went everywhere together—they were inseparable. News conferences were no exception, and at one of them President Coolidge interrupted the questioning when he heard the plaintive whining of the collie.

"Will you newspapermen," bellowed the angry Chief Executive, "kindly keep your big feet off my dog's toes!"

The dog also whined, on another occasion but for a different reason. The occasion was a breakfast at the White House to which dignitaries had been invited. In one of the chairs at the table sat Senator Sheppard of Texas; on the floor beside him sat Rob Roy, whining and shaking his head.

"What's wrong with this dog?" asked Sheppard.

"Wrong? Nothing's wrong," replied President Coolidge. "He wants your bacon."

The shocked and chagrined Senator, realizing that Coolidge fully expected him to appease the dog, diplomatically fed Rob Roy his only slice of bacon.

Like Presidents Roosevelt, Johnson, and Coolidge, the modern-day pet owner loves his pet and does his best to see that the pet is cared for. This fact can have quite humorous ramifications.

People who are city dwellers must put up with a great many pressures and irritants that can lead to mild disorders or even severe mental breakdowns. To prevent this from happening, people employ a variety of actions ranging from biofeedback sessions and psychiatric counseling to merely buying a six-pack of beer and going out to carouse or spending a quiet evening at home.

Of course, the fast pace of city living can have its effects on pets as well as their human companions. Recognizing this fact, a Mr. Shigenori Nasuda, owner of a Tokyo pet shop, began a new service recently to help pets cope with the pressures of metropolitan living.

"Pets can go crazy living in a city like Tokyo," said Shigenori. His answer was to offer yoga instruction for the pets. "This can help your pet unwind, relax, and be whole again," he explained.

Dr. Michael Fox, a U.S. veterinarian and author of several bestselling pet books, would undoubtedly agree. In 1981, his book on how to massage one's pet was published.

While yoga and massage for pets may seem a little too much, the success of the endeavors of Mr. Nasuda and the popularity of Dr. Fox's book graphically demonstrate the emergence of pets in the world of people.

In fact, pets are so popular and in such demand today that even fantasy pets are in vogue. In Austin, Texas, the innovative manager of a large shopping mall recently generated a lot of interest among children by sponsoring, in conjunction with the city's parks and recreation department, an "Invisible Pet Show." In a newspaper account of the show Kevin Farrell of Highland Mall stated that, "By the 1980 census there are

A Tokyo pet shop recently began offering a new service to help pets cope with the stress of metropolitan life—yoga classes.

an estimated 6,000 invisible pets living in Austin. Of course," quipped Farrell, "I haven't seen them."

The sponsors invited children to bring their invisible pets to the mall. Each entrant had a few minutes to show his pet and have it perform any special feat or trick it could do. The feat was to be limited only by the child's imagination. Invisible props were allowed. Kids were warned that their unseeable pet would have to be talented, well-groomed, and well-behaved "to have even a ghost of a chance." And finally, entrants were advised that invisible messes should be cleaned up before leaving the mall.

Now, who can keep a straight face when reading of such happenings? Are such activities frivolous? Perhaps. But, again, they are in no way harmful, and provide a wealth of fun and entertainment. Whatever pet lovers may be accused of, it certainly is not lack of a sense of humor!

It has been our experience that pet lovers are no different than other folks. Maybe they are a little more intelligent and kind-hearted. And perhaps they do have a more well-developed sense of humor (the authors are a bit prejudiced), but other than that, they are like average people on the street.

THE PET LOVER

Because pet lovers are often castigated as being frivolous and silly, maybe we should take a look at some typical people who appreciate pets, just to get a view of what kind of person pampers pets.

There is little Kim Scott, 5 years old, of Lake Charles, Louisiana. Kim says her kitten, Gingham, is "smarter than anything."

"She sleeps with me every night," says the cute, blue-eyed Kim, "but my parents don't know it. They don't like Gingham to sleep in my bed, so I sneak her in."

Bob Whisenant of St. Louis, a captain in the Army stationed at Fort Lewis, Washington, says his German shepherd dog, Tanko, is his "best friend."

19

"My wife Linda travels a lot as a representative of a pharmaceutical company," explains Bob. "She's gone several days at a time and good ol' Tanko sure is a lot of company then."

Joyce Carter, a housewife in Beaumont, Texas, claims her dog Fluffy, a solid white mix, is a "real friend and companion."

"The first thing my husband Philip does when he comes home from work each day," says Joyce, "is to hug and pet Fluffy. The second thing is to do the same to me."

Merle Haggard, noted country music singer and two-time winner of the Country Music Entertainer of the Year Award, cared so much for his female toy terrier, WaWe, that he cancelled a concert tour for his dog. WaWe always accompanies Merle along with the other members of his traveling road show. While on a tour of the Southeast, the toy terrier gave birth to pups. Merle, who had been saddened previously because another beloved pet had died, stopped the tour so the health of the new mom and her pups was not jeopardized. Later, a photo of WaWe and her "dad," Merle Haggard, were featured on the cover of one of his hit albums.

Kim, Bob, Joyce, Merle, and millions of other nice people own and love pets. These people are neither eccentric nor silly. They are simply everyday Americans who believe that their pet dogs or cats are important parts of their—and their family's—lives.

Families and individuals with socially rich lives and a vast array of friends and loved ones often find that a pet adds just that little extra bit of fun and love to their lives. A happy-go-lucky pet can add spice and variety to an already content, well-adjusted family. In such an instance, the family pet is the icing on the cake of a satisfying network of human relationships.

CHAPTER 2

WHAT'S IN A NAME?

THE SIGNIFICANCE OF NAMES

The naming of a pet by the human "parent" is a special event. A name, after all, is not *just* a name. It is a word (or words) that give meaning to one's existence in this world. A name accords special recognition to a person—or a pet.

Throughout history, names have been considered of great significance. The Romans attached incredible importance to a person's name. Roman numerologists, for example, claimed they could divine the future of a person by assigning numbers to his or her name.

In the Bible one also finds much ado being made over the giving of names. In the book of Genesis, for instance, God changed Abram's name to Abraham, which means "father of nations." This change emphasizes the importance of a name in terms of truly describing the person and providing direct and purposeful meaning.

On the opposite end of the scale is the number 666 given in the book of Revelation of the New Testament to the great satanic dictator who is to rise to power in the last days.

A name's significance has even been found to have an impact on how others react to and treat a person. In a class-room study of teacher attitudes and behavior, it was found that children with unpopular names (for example, Alma, Bertha, Mortimer, or Elmer) were given less attention and were considered "less intelligent" by their teachers than children with more popular names.

A name signifies that a person or creature is important and has certain unalienable rights while on earth. That is why it is well understood that failure to recognize another's name is to imply that the unrecognized person is somehow sub-human or unworthy of name recognition. Thus, prisoners in a penitentiary or jail are given numbers and not names, military boot camp trainees are assigned serial numbers, and concentration camp Jews in Nazi Germany were addressed by a number or a racial epithet rather than by their proper names.

Thus, we can state with certainty that names are of vital importance and meaning. A name provides a stamp of recognition to a person or creature—a statement of individuality or singleness.

In the context of pet names, we find that pets (first the dog, than later the cat) probably were given names as soon as they were first domesticated. But unlike sheep or cattle, creatures such as the dog and cat were not tamed *per se* by man. Instead, they voluntarily joined the family of man. And when these special creatures joined man and became loyal and loving pets, the practice of assigning names to them was the most natural thing for the human members of the family to do.

HISTORY AND CUSTOM OF ASSIGNING NAMES

No one knows for sure when man first gave names to pets. Of course, one finds in the Bible that Adam first named all the animals and beasts that God made. It makes you wonder what names he selected. But probably, this passage in Genesis refers to the designation of species, types, or breeds (canine, tiger, snake, or whatever) rather than the giving of personal names.

Most likely, the first time an animal domesticated by man was named was in the days of the cavemen. About 15,000 years ago, in Central and North Asia, dogs were first domesticated. Indeed, the term *domesticus* means "to cast one's lot with man."

Dogs cast their lot with man because it was advantageous for them to do so. First, they were probably scavengers, for it was no doubt easier to scavenge through garbage heaps for animal remains left by man than to stalk and kill one's own food. It seems reasonable to assume that the scavenger dogs soon befriended man and became loyal, devoted companions. And it is also reasonable to assume that the cavemen and women gave their new-found friends individual names.

In this prehistoric era men were given names which signified physical characteristics (Strong Warrior or Tall One), or names that coincided with an event in nature (Thunder Cloud or Running Brook). It is likely that their new pets were likewise given names based on similar criteria. This parallel still exists in contemporary times. For example, the modern names Spunky, Speedy, Rocky, Blue, Lightning, or Blacky signify either a physical trait or an attribute of nature.

Compared to canines, cats are relative newcomers to the family of man. History records that cats were first domesticated in Egypt 3600 years ago during the Stone Age. Historians theorize that farming by man caught the attention of the cats, for wherever there was grain in the fields, there were mice. So the cats came for the mice and eventually took up with the farmers and their families.

Thus the feline, like his counterpart, the dog, voluntarily cast his lot with man. He was not forced to do so, and no yoke nor fence was required to keep him. Instead, cats took up with people, wisely recognizing the advantages of such an association.

Interestingly, the Egyptians held the cat in high regard. In fact, cats were deemed to be gods and goddesses. Temples were dedicated to felines and the punishment for harming a cat was instant death.

In 1861 at Beni Hasan, Egypt, the British unearthed a cat cemetery. What they found boggled the mind. Over 89,000 cat mummies were found, complete with ornate and elaborate mummy cases. In each mummy case was a much smaller mummy case, containing—what else?—a mouse or shrew, obviously intended for the dead cat's dining pleasure in the next world!

The Egyptians assigned names to their cats. Symbolic of the cat deity was *Pasht,* a feline-looking idol that signified fertility and love in Egyptian mythology and religion. Many experts believe that from this name was derived the modern

"Puss" or "Pussy" that often serves as another informal term for cat.

Both cats and dogs have gone through times of great respect and admiration and through periods when they were vilified and ostracized from the human family. Generally, in the modern era, cats and dogs have consistently achieved positive status in the affairs of men in the overall scheme of society.

Cats probably have a more illustrious background, at least in terms of endurance and ages-old respect. Cats have been admired for centuries by the most educated and renowned leaders of the world. Confucius, for instance, in 500 B.C. favored a cat for a personal pet. The Prophet Mohammed was also a great lover and admirer of cats. Although he loved all felines, Mohammed's most beloved pet was a white cat which he named "Muezza." He was so struck with cats that Mohammed often preached with a cat in his hands, stroking its fur as he regaled the multitudes with his oratory.

About the same time in Japan, cats began to be kept in temples to guard sacred manuscripts. Robed monks and priests gave names to their temple watchcats, such as "Keeper of Light" and "Guardian Eyes," which were in accord with their role as protector of the sacred scrolls.

To the west of Japan in China, dogs found popularity during the Middle Ages, not only as household pets but also for hunting. Marco Polo's writings tell of the Great Khan of the Tartars conducting a hunt preceded by over 5,000 yelping dogs.

China is also unique in that it was there that pigs gained some measure of popularity as household pets. This popularity stemmed from the advice of ancient Chinese philosophers that people should "shave a pig and take him to bed." There was a good reason for this unusual bit of advice. The northern region of China got bitterly cold in the winter, and the people suffered because they had no heat for their homes and precious few bed covers. So they began taking their porker friends to bed with them. The pigs' warm bodies kept the people warm. There was only one problem—the sharp bristles on the faces of the pigs caused many a sleepless night. The solution, of course, was to shave the pigs' faces.

A few centuries earlier in Europe, dogs became very fashionable with royalty and aristocratic nobles. King Canute of Denmark, for instance, pampered the dogs he used for hunting. He set aside thousands of acres for their domicile, and he ordered that stray dogs, who unknowingly wandered onto the domain of the royal dogs, have their legs broken! Obviously, like many people today, the King loved those of his own family, but not those outside the clan.

Even then, the pleasures of owning a pet were often tempered by the misfortunes that sometimes occurred. In November of 1660, for example, the *Mercurius Politicus,* a paper published in London, England, carried a lost dog ad placed by none other than King Charles II. Charles, later to be roundly criticized by many historians as self-indulgent, a wastrel, and a blight upon the throne, was, nevertheless, a compassionate and tender-hearted soul when it came to his beloved dog.

In the ad, Charles stated that someone had stolen his dog, and he wanted it back. The dog was described as black and a cross between a spaniel and a greyhound. According to the ad, the dog "was better known at court than those who stole him." Added the frustrated leader of the far-flung British Empire, "Will they never leave robbing his majesty? Must he not keep a dog?" This ad in the tiny London newspaper (about the size of a sheet of stationery today) is the only paper in which a member of royalty is known to have advertised—and it was for a lost dog!

It was about a hundred years after the reign of Charles II that the Earl of Bridgewater, Francis Egerton (1756-1829), came to be known as the most unusual pet fancier of all time. The Earl owned a variety of dogs, all of whom received his doting attention. He dressed all the dog members of his family in people clothes, including handsome leather boots. They were required to report promptly to the Earl's table for dinner each night where they sat in armchairs, draped with freshly starched napkins around their necks. The canines were attended by human servants who served them food from sterling silver serving dishes. But woe to the hapless dog who violated table manners! Those who breached the Earl's dinner etiquette were banished from the table and forced to eat alone.

Queen Victoria of England (1819-1901) also had a passion for dogs. The first royal act Victoria performed following her coronation was to wash one of her favored canines. The Queen owned 83 dogs, and she had no problem remembering each of their names.

Names for pets in Queen Victoria's time generally were coined from some physical or personal characteristic. Ray, for example, meant "red-haired"; Ripley was derived from an Anglo Saxon name meaning "the shouter"; and Truman, which in Old English meant "Faithful." Sometimes, however, the pet was named after another animal he resembled. For example, fox-like canines might be called Russell, an Old English name for a red fox; or Wolfe, a Teutonic word which means to be cunning, wise, and brave. Cats sometimes were named Chad, meaning wildcat or fighting warrior. Also, there was Fleta (Teutonic for the fleet or swift), Fiona (Celtic for white or fair), and Flavia (Latin for blond or yellow-haired).

In France, popular poodle names included Fifi and Idette. Fifi, interestingly enough, is an off-shoot of the word Josephine and also means "he shall add" (Fifine) in Hebrew. Idette is a name of Teutonic origin meaning "happy little one."

In any discussion of French names, one must not omit that of Bleu. Bleu (Blue in English) was the favorite dog of King Louis IX of France. This hapless pet's name is probably best remembered today in its most irreverent form—that of a curseword or swear term.

It seems that King Louis was a very pious man who detested foul language by his courtiers. Therefore, he ordered that those heard using profanity have their tongues branded with a hot iron.

The noble ladies and men of the court, not wishing to have their tongues seared, used the ruse of making the name of the King's dog a byword. Thus, today, two of the more popular cursewords in French are *Sacre Bleu!* (Holy Blue) and *Par Bleu!* (for Blue).

King Louis IX's grandfather, King Louis VII, also had an abiding love for dogs. It is said that even when he was near

26

his death, unable to move and contorted by pain, he happily spent the last hours of his life watching his dogs hunting and catching mice in the royal bedroom.

Cats were also highly regarded by the French. During the reign of King Louis XV, the royal courtiers poured perfume on his white cat, a Persian breed, leading his majesty to complain about the waste of good perfume. Nevertheless, the ladies of the nobility continued the sweet-smelling practice.

It was in France in the 1600s that the noted French philosopher Montaigne made one of the most profound statements ever recorded about the thoughts and behavior of pets. Observing his own enthusiastic pleasure as well as that of his cat as they engaged in play, Montaigne wrote, "When I play with my cat, who knows whether she does not amuse herself more with me than I do with her?"

However, one cannot accuse the 17th and 18th century French of narrowmindedly relying on the companionship of cats and dogs alone. Among the upper classes, a wide-ranging assortment of pets was the fashion.

The famed French author Alexander Dumas *(The Three Musketeers* and *The Count of Monte Cristo)* had a pet vulture which he christened Jurgatha, the meaning of which we have been unable to find in the course of our research. In any case, Dumas enjoyed his activities with Jurgatha immensely. He taught the bird many tricks and each Sunday dutifully took the bird for a walk down the *Champs E'lysees.* Ladies and gentlemen walking their pet poodles down the wide avenue were astonished to see Dumas strolling merrily by with Jurgatha hopping along behind on a silver leash.

Other French words for pets passed down from the era of nobility are Bouffant (fluffy), Bijou (friendly), Blanche (white and fair), Midget (petite), and Dominic (Sunday's child).

The American experience in naming pets shows a wide variety of ways to distinguish the loved one. For example, a study of the names of pets owned by presidents shows that names were given based on location, physical and personality traits, people's names, and even military rank

(The General, the name of one of John Tyler's most beloved horses).

Andrew Jackson had two horses, for example, named Lady Nashville and Bolivia (location); Ulysses Grant named his horse Jeff Davis, after Grant's Civil War adversary; Teddy Roosevelt called his sneaky housecat Slippers; and Calvin Coolidge named his black chow Blackberry. Franklin Roosevelt humorously named his huge English sheepdog Tiny, and John Kennedy oddly nicknamed his canary Robin. Kennedy also had a cat named Tom Kitten and a dog called Wolf.

If you got a good chuckle from the story of the Chinese taking pigs to bed to keep warm, consider the drama of pets in American history. The biographies of Abraham Lincoln reveal that as a boy he had a pig for a pet, which he rode just like other boys rode horses. And later, when he was president, the Lincoln children slept in the White House with their favorite pet, Nanny, a goat. Andrew Jackson dearly loved his parrot, Poor Poll, and William Taft, who became president in 1909, let his pet cow, Pauline, chomp on the lush grass of the White House lawn.

The distinguished Benjamin Franklin was another who believed that pets served a greater purpose than just being the footstool of man. Franklin was so touched when Mungo, a squirrel owned by a friend, escaped from his cage and was killed by a neighbor's dog that he wrote the following letter to the friend, Georgianna Shipley:

London, September 26, 1772
I lament with you most sincerely the unfortunate end of poor Mungo. Few squirrels were better accomplished; for he had had a good education, had travelled far, and seen much of the world. As he had the honour of being, for his virtues, your favourite, he should not go, like common skuggs, without an elegy or an epitaph. Let us give him one in the monumental style and measure, which, being neither prose nor verse, is perhaps the properest for grief; since to use common language would look as if we were not affected, and to make rhymes would seem trifling in sorrow.

EPITAPH

Alas! poor Mungo
Happy wert thou, hadst thou known
Thy own felicity.
Remote from the fierce bald eagle,
Tyrant of thy native woods,
Thou hadst nought to fear from his piercing talons,
Nor from the murdering gun
Of the thoughtless sportsman.
Safe in thy wired castle,
Grimalkin never could annoy thee.

Daily wert thou fed with the choicest viands,
By the fair hand of an indulgent mistress;
But, discontented,
Thou wouldst have more freedom.
Too soon, alas! didst thou obtain it;
And wandering,
Thou art fallen by the fangs of wanton, cruel Ranger!

Learn hence,
Ye who blindly seek more liberty,
Whether subjects, sons, squirrels or daughters,
That apparent restraint may be real protection;
Yielding peace and plenty
With security

You see, my dear Miss, how much more decent and proper this broken style is, than if we were to say, by way of epitaph,

Here Skugg
Lies snug,
As a bug
In a rug.

and yet, perhaps, there are people in the world of so little feeling as to think that this would be a good-enough epitaph for poor Mungo.

PET NAMES FOR MODERN TIMES

Many of the names handed down to us from history are still popular, but each day brings a totally new and unique assortment of pet names as people who acquire pets seek that perfect name for their own special pet. And so today, pet names show a diversity and breadth which defy classification. It seems that people are much more conservative in assigning names to their human children than they are to their pets. Some of the most humorous, wacky, and bizarre names imaginable are fixed on hapless pets by Americans. On the other hand, some of the names given pets reflect a degree of beauty, warmth, and significance unreflected in the names of humans.

In any event, the names available for pets seem endless. Our list in this book is only a smattering of the countless possibilities open to the human parents of a newly acquired pet, although we believe it to be the most comprehensive and worthwhile list to be found anywhere.

However, before you proceed on to the names in the list (maybe you have already taken a peek—we couldn't blame you!), we would like to offer some additional advice and information which will make your task of finding that "just right" name for your pet more fun and rewarding. In the following chapter we hope to shed some light on the factors you may wish to consider in making your choice.

For example, should you select a name based on a special meaning derived from historical roots? Might your pet be named after a famous pet hero or heroine, or maybe in honor of a town or city whose memory you cherish? Perhaps your pet's name can be derived from adjectives based on his physical characteristics or personality traits. As we will discuss next, there are a variety of methods you can use in devining the perfect name for your pet.

CHAPTER 3

HOW TO SELECT THE RIGHT NAME

BEAUTY IS IN THE EYE OF THE BEHOLDER

So you now have a new member in your family. We are sure you are as proud of the new arrival as he or she is of becoming a part of your life.

It is an interesting fact that there is not a universal pet that is perfect for everyone. Some people like cats, some do not. Many adore canines, many others do not. One friend of ours says she would have nothing but Siamese cats; another friend swears by the Persian breed of feline. People's taste in pets is just as variable as is their taste in human companions.

Another consideration is that of age. Some prefer a young puppy or kitten, while others desire a more mature pet.

The fact that there are so many breeds and types of pets of varying ages makes the selection and adoption of a pet an interesting and fun affair. But whatever pet you choose, he or she must be christened with a name.

However, not just any name will do. The new family member definitely needs a name which will *perfectly* describe his or her personality and physical features. At the same time, keep in mind that you, the proud and happy parents of this new addition to the family, also have an important stake in the name selected. It must be psychologically and aesthetically satisfying to you so that each time you pronounce it you will feel delighted and contented that the name chosen "fits" your own psyche and personality "like a glove."

Of course it is obvious that if you detest a certain name, or if it dredges up thoughts in your mind that are unsettling or distasteful, you should instantly discard the name as an option. Just as beauty is in the eye of the beholder, so the impact of a name is significant for the individual. What to me or another person is a positively fitting, even charming, name for your pet may be totally unacceptable to you. This is understandable and to be taken into account.

The key rule in naming your pet is this: select a name which is ideal for your pet *and* ideal for you. Remember, you and your pet will *both* have to live with this name for many years to come—for the pet, all of his or her life!

In this chapter we will discuss some of the more important factors you should consider in picking out that "just right" name for your pet. We will also discuss some worthwhile methods and techniques you might use to select a name.

FACTORS TO CONSIDER

There are as many factors and reasons to consider in giving a particular name to a pet as there are types and breeds of pets. Let us consider some of the most crucial.

Select One Name Only

It is surprising, but true, that many people call their pets by two or more names. In one amusing instance, a lady told us her white cat had two names. "You see," she explained, "my cat's astrological sign is Gemini. That's two personalities, you know. Sometimes she's good and behaves, so I call her Miss Goodhead. Other times she can be devilish and cranky. That's when I call her Miss Meany Ears!" Gemini or not, her cat, especially as a young kitten, was no doubt sometimes a little confused over the two labels she had to recognize.

Human beings are sometimes saddled with two names, too. Parents will assign a formal name to the child, then later add a nickname. For instance, back in her school days, Wanda recalls a young man named Robert. As a tyke, Robert's hair was so platinum blond and whitish his mother began to call him "Cotton." Later, as his hair grew darker, she switched to

Robert. But sometimes she slipped and reverted back to calling him Cotton. Understandably, poor Robert often was bewildered.

A pet should have one name and one name only. To call a cat Tiger one day, because of his yellow tabby stripes, and by his formal name Elmer or Slippers the next, can confuse and disorient the poor creature.

Most pets can overcome the handicap of being called two names, but why present an obstacle to their development? There are so many nice names available. Surely, one (and one only) can be found.

Interestingly, we have run across cases in which a pet became confused when, even though he or she had a single name, it was *pronounced* differently by people. For instance, a couple who owned a lovely white terrier named Sasha (pronounced Sah-sha) left the dog in the care of the husband's mother for a month while they went on an extended vacation overseas. When they returned, the mother complained that the dog refused to mind and never came when called. "I kept pleading with her, come here Say-sha, but she wouldn't budge."

Pronunciation may seem only a small consideration, but an anecdote once told by President Reagan is instructive on the problem of mispronouncing a name. In this case, the name was his own.

"When I was first running for office and wasn't well-known, this gentleman was preparing to introduce me at a luncheon in New York the next day," said Reagan. "The man tossed in bed trying to figure out if the candidate's name was pronounced Ree-gan or Ray-gun. Finally he got up and went for a walk, and ran into a friend who was out exercising his dog. He explained his problem. The friend asked whether the candidate was Irish. Told he was, the friend declared, 'It's Ray-gun. I guarantee it. I know how those Irishmen pronounce their names. It's definitely Ray-gun.'

"The gentleman expressed his thanks, then admired the dog and asked what kind it was. 'Thank you,' said the friend. 'It's a bagel'."

To Fit Personality

One of the more popular methods people use to name their pet is to select the name for a trait that is most prominent in the pet's personality.

If your dog is a real cut-up, you could dub him Clown. Or how about Rascal if he is very mischievous? If your cat is finicky or snooty and thinks she is superior to other cats, how would a name like Queen or Duchess fit?

Both nouns and adjectives can be used to label a pet with a name that is indicative of his or her temperament and personality. For instance, consider these nouns:

Angel (or Devil)	King
Cricket	Lance
Hawk	Dolly
Sweetstuff	Duke
Ginger	Turtle
Sugar	Rifle
Possum	Saint
President	

Many more possibilities are found in our comprehensive list later in this book.

Some adjectives that may fit are:

Spunky	Sweet
Crabby	Frosty
Cranky	Sparky
Happy	Messy

To use personality as a method, all you have to do is carefully consider the behavior pattern and idiosyncrasies of your pet. Like people, every pet has a distinctive and unique personality.

A colleague of ours told an entertaining story of how her dog used his slyness and intelligence to gain attention. One day, the dog saw a sandcrab running on the ground and proceeded to chase and snap at it. To his dismay, its claws fastened on his tender snoot and he gave a loud yelp. Everyone came running and, seeing him in pain, offered solace and comfort to the dog, stroking his fur and telling him he would be all right. All this attention was, naturally, highly pleasing to the pet.

After that, whenever the dog felt neglected, he would let out the same big yelp and paw at his nose, pretending a sand-crab had again gotten him!

Also, to attract attention, the clever dog began to feign a leg injury. When people were not around, he was spry, ener-getic, and physically fit. But in the presence of people, he would limp and favor his right front paw. After his human family and friends realized what he was doing, the shenanigans of their pet became a great source of amusement to them.

The moral of the story: the dog's name had been Blake; however, after he began to compete for an Academy Award his name was changed to Oscar for his superb acting ability. Very appropriate!

This leads us to consider another factor. Should a pet's name, once given, be *changed*?

Changing a Name

Although it is not a good idea to change the name of your pet, there are situations when this is either advisable or necessary. One instance may be when a name no longer fits the pet. If, for example, you made the mistake of naming your cuddly, small puppy Teeny-bits or Tiny, and now, at maturity, he's a raging, giant bull of a dog, maybe a name change is in order. Of course, if you select a proper name initially, such problems need not arise.

But say you have adopted a grown pet who has obviously been slapped with a most unbecoming *nom de plume*. Under such a circumstance, would it be wise to change the pet's name? Perhaps.

The wife of Calvin Coolidge, American president during the 1920s, came upon such a circumstance during her stay at the White House. Mrs. Coolidge was crazy about pets. She

"Butch, this job's gonna be a breeze . . . I understand all the
lady's got is a mutt named Tiny."

turned the White House and its grounds into a virtual zoo. She enjoyed immensely the task of naming her pets and chose the names with both precision and an eye for humor. A pair of canaries she named Nip and Tuck. Two cats were called Blacky and Tiger. She dubbed a pet raccoon Rebecca, a chow dog Blackberry, and a delicate collie Prudence Prim.

When the White House acquired pets which already had names, Mrs. Coolidge normally kept the names they were given. But, the personalities of two pets seemed to cry out for name changes.

The first case was that of Laddie Buck, an Airedale dog. After only a few days in his new surroundings, Mrs. Coolidge changed his name to Paul Pry because he was continually prying into every corner of the White House. Paul Pry was the nosiest dog, said Mrs. Coolidge, that she had ever seen.

The next case was that of Rob Roy, a gorgeous white collie. His original name was Oshkosh, after the town of Oshkosh, Wisconsin, where the dog was born, but the dog proved to be so frisky and energetic and such a rascal that Mrs. Coolidge decided to seek a new, more appropriate name. She came up with Rob Roy, after an outlaw bandit in a novel by Englishman Sir Walter Scott. Rob Roy was a little confused at first over the name change, but he soon took to it and became *the* favorite White House pet.

Rob Roy went everywhere with the president and made the acquaintance of many foreign heads of state and other distinguished visitors. All commented that he seemed to be a perfect representative of America: he was friendly, enthusiastic, and devoted to his family. Just a good, solid, all-American kid!

In many cultures, the names of young men or women are changed at puberty. This signifies that the young person is shedding his youthful behaviors and immaturity and taking on the responsibilities of adulthood. For example, a custom of the Indian tribes of North America was to change young warriors' names to reflect the more masculine, adult role expected of them as they passed the age of puberty.

Regardless of these customs in some human societies, it probably is not a good idea to change the name of a pet except for a meaningful reason. If such a reason exists, a name change can be made with only minor difficulty by the simple method used to teach a pet any valuable new lesson: association with behavioral rewards. A food treat periodically offered the pet and given to him when he responds to your calling him by his new name will usually serve to train him to accept the new title. Naturally, the old name you wish to discard should be totally withdrawn from the pet's environment, so he does not become confused by hearing it.

To Fit Physical Characteristics

If the pet's physical attributes are charmingly skewed in one aspect, a name based on physical characteristics can be irresistible. For instance, the name Curly for a cockapoo, Fluffy for a Persian cat, Slinky for a ferret, or simply Pug for a pug bulldog. However, as mentioned earlier, the owner must take care not to assign a name based on size or juvenile behavior that will most certainly need revision when the pet reaches maturity. Cutestuff, Sweetpea, or Two-bits may seem wonderfully precious names for a small cuddly Newfoundland or chow puppy, but after a year or so, they will not do.

If you wish to use a name suggested by physical stature, any problem that might come up in the future can easily be alleviated by a little foresight and good judgment. Just envision your sweet kitten or puppy *next year.* If your kitten is of that rare breed that reaches 25 or 30 pounds, or your puppy is a German shepherd, a Great Dane, or St. Bernard, then discretion is in order.

Some examples of names to fit physical characteristics are:

Velvet or Satiny (for soft, smooth fur or hair)

Leather, Rough, or Wrinkles (for hairless types, or the incredible Chinese Sharpei dog that has more wrinkles than body!)

Sandy, Goldy, or Yeller (if the color matches)

Big Boy or Shorty	Whitey
Giant	Stumpy
Choppers (big teeth)	Snow
Kettle (if black)	Smoothie
Drum	Jaws
Red	Slowpoke
Blacky	Speedy

The last two names mentioned could also fit into the category of *personality* traits. The slow gait of a pet turtle would be based on the physical, while the behavior of a dog that is slow and meandering might be caused by his psychological disposition. A greyhound, for example, might be called Speedy due to his physical talent and a small Pekingnese might deserve the same title due to his hyperactive personality.

The use of a pet's physical attributes to suggest a name can, however, backfire if not used with care. This can happen if the term selected is in some way derogatory. This leads us to the factor of psychology.

The Psychological Factor

Earlier in this book we mentioned that studies have shown how people's perception of names can lead to conclusions and, eventually, behaviors and attitudes that are totally unintended. In psychology, this is called the *Pygmalion Effect.*

Take the names of people, for instance. A name like Agatha or Fauntleroy can give a child a lot of agony in life. So can Ada, Ethyl, and Casper. There is nothing intrinsically wrong with these names. At one time they were all extremely fashionable. But times change—and so does fashion in names. To plant one of these names on a young child today is, to say the least, an act of unthinking cruelty.

This fact is based on the negative way people view or perceive these names. If, for instance, people associate the name Agatha with old-fashioned and out of date, straitlaced women, the danger is that they might impart to a contemporary young girl named Agatha these same ideas or perceptions.

Names have magic, both for those who have them and those who say them. For example, which person would you suspect is more intellectual and aristocratic: Robert Wood Bentley, or Bob Bentley? Obviously, the added dimension of how we perceive a name makes a big difference.

How does this fact relate to pet names? Well, let us go back to the name Speedy or Slowpoke, terms selected perhaps due to the personality characteristic of the pet. Psychological experts suggest to us that if you *expect* a person to act in a certain way, this often is a self-fulfilling prophecy and he or she will begin to act as expected.

If you call your dog Speedy, your voice tone can be expected to coincide with the use of this term. You would not normally call out "Speedy, come here" in a slow, deliberate drawl, would you? No. Instead, it would be a snappy tone. And your pet will act accordingly.

I once knew a man who called his dog "Ugly." And amazingly, the poor dog acted like he was a mangy, unattractive mutt. He rarely would come when called, and he appeared unhappy and withdrawn. Maybe this can be explained by his master's behavior. Believing his dog to be ugly and physically unappealing, he acted toward the dog in exactly that manner. This was apparent even in the owner's tone of voice. Instead of a happy and delightful sound, the word "Ugly" came out in a snarled, disrespectful sort of way.

I brought this to the owner's attention, and he was startled. He explained that when he first acquired Ugly, the dog had a disease which caused most of his hair to fall out. Some of the hair was still missing. Because the dog was unkempt in appearance, he chose the name Ugly. "I didn't intend to make the dog feel bad," he said.

When we claim that names can affect behavior, even in pets, we are not implying that a pet can perfectly understand the linquistic meaning or definition of a word (like Ugly). The pet may not understand the definition of a word, but most pets—dogs and cats in particular—are intelligent and perceptive enough to pick up on the way people *act* toward them. It is the people who use the name, and the manner in which they say and use it, that causes the pet to react negatively or positively.

Since name usage may actually cause a behavioral problem, names should be carefully chosen to preclude such an outcome. Perhaps Slowpoke is a good name, if the pet's manner reflects this behavior. Flash or Speedy, likewise, may be highly descriptive of some pets. If you choose names like these, make sure the term you select is indicative of the *good* behavior you wish the pet to exhibit.

Instead of negatively charged names, consider the positive aspect of names like:

Grace	Brighty
Beauty	Pretty Boy
Sugar	Valiant
Noble	Courageous
Smart	Divine

Our lists in Chapter 5 offer many others you may consider.

To Fit Breed

One interesting way to pick a name is to select a term derived from the pet's breed. There are several ways to do this.

One way is to choose a term that characterizes the unique or special behavior of a specific breed. For instance, one man gave his Basenji dog the name "Cat," a title obviously out of character, even odd, for a canine. However, it is not so odd if one knows something about the Basenji, for this is the only breed of dog that cleans itself by licking all over its body with its tongue. Unfortunately, few people know this unusual fact and so the beleaguered owner of Cat is continually met with strange looks or laughter when he introduces his Basenji dog to strangers.

Many other examples can be found. The famed author Lord Byron dubbed his Newfoundland dog Boatswain, a highly appropriate name for a dog like the Newfoundland, which has rescued many hapless, shipwrecked victims from Canada's icy North Atlantic waters.

A gentleman friend of ours named his English bulldog Matador (Spanish for bullfighter). The reason, he explained,

41

is that this breed was used in Europe for many years in the fighting of bulls. In fact, the distinctive, flat nose of the English bulldog was designed for combat, the result of generations of hybrid breeding. The flat nose allowed the fighting dog to grab hold of a bull's neck without worrying about his snout getting in the way.

However, it should be noted that Matador has totally forgotten his ancestry. When any visitor arrives, he quickly skips away to hide behind the nearest piece of furniture. I am quite sure that this peaceful English bulldog would die of fright if he ever directly confronted a charging bull.

Another way to use breed as a basis for a name is to capture the spirit of the nation or region of the world where the breed first originated. The common use of French names for poodles exemplifies this technique. Fifi, Bridget, Louis, Pierre, Marie, Lorraine, Paris, and Champagne are examples.

If you have a Siamese cat, you may wish to call her Bangkok or Siam, or perhaps you might choose a Thai name:

Sangkhla (water festival)	Layo Layo (fast)
Suhway (beautiful)	Nitnoy (small one)

For an Irish wolfhound there is Patrick, Dublin, Greenie, or Clover.

If you have a Scandinavian breed dog, a Norwegian elkhound, Great Dane, Swedish elkhound, or spitz, there are the names Oslo, Erik, Erika, Thor, Thora, Lars, and Olaf.

If you have a dog of English origin such as the foxhound, springer spaniel, beagle, or the Shetland sheepdog, you would probably enjoy names like London, Winchester, Dover, Cardiff, Lord, Buck (for Buckingham), Windsor, and Churchill.

There is also Lancelot, Prescott, Roderick, and Merlin. And, wouldn't a Scotch terrier feel good about Plaid, or Checkers, Kilt, or Bagpipe?

German breeds such as German shepherds, Pomeranians, Weimaraners, Dobermans, and Schnauzers deserve names like Munich, Konrad, Bismarck, Berlin, Ingrid, Otto, Fritz, Helga, Hansel, or Gretel.

For Russian breeds like the Borzoi, the Russian wolfhound dog, or the Russian blue cat, there are Ivan, Czar, and Bolshoi.

Names for Abysinnian cats, whose ancestry traces back to ancient Egypt, include Cairo, Tunis, Pyramid, Cleopatra, and King Tut.

Then there are the oriental breeds. Is yours a lovely Persian cat? How about the simple but beautiful, Persia, or, perhaps, Teheran, Shah, Cambyses, or Jasmine.

Names such as Orient, Rangoon, Malay, and Singapore may fit the Birman and Burmese cats quite nicely. Nepal, Manchu, Shanghai, Peking, Confucius, and Yalu may be fitting names for Tibetan spaniels, the Chinese Sharpei, and the Pekingnese dogs. For the Manx cat which, the story goes, came from Spain, perhaps Madrid or Lady Spain would be suitable.

As you can see, the list is endless if you wish to use geographical flavor to guide your selection of a name. Only the outer limits of your imagination preclude you from finding that one best name from among the virtual sea of names that flood this fruitful category.

After Famous Pets and Animals

Some parents name their pets after famous pets and animal celebrities such as Lassie, Rin Tin Tin, Morris, Benji, Garfield, or Boomer. If you wish to take this approach, there are countless possibilities listed in this book. Our list includes famous movie and television stars, pets—real or fictional— from books and cartoon series, and hero/heroine animals. The latter group includes names of those who have won acclaim for heroic actions—saving people's lives, for instance, or thwarting a robbery. In the case of horses, it includes the names of champion thoroughbreds who have won the Kentucky Derby, Belmont Stakes, and the Preakness races.

The list is quite large. There are:

Cleo (from the old George Burns/Gracie Allen comedy series)

Snoopy (dog in *Peanuts* cartoon by Schultz)

Marmaduke (another cartoon character)

Citation (renowned race horse)

Francis (the talking mule of movie fame)

Fury (beloved horse from children's books and movie)

Not as well-known, but certainly deserving of mention are hero pets like Greyfriars Bobby, an unusually loyal Skye terrier who stayed by his master's grave for ten years after the master's death, and Bari, the legendary Saint Bernard dog who rescued forty-four persons from almost certain deaths in the rugged Alps. Sadly, Bari was killed in his attempt to rescue a forty-fifth person in distress. During a raging blizzard, the man to be rescued mistook Bari for a bear and shot him.

Dogs such as Bobby, Bari, and others—like the legendary Lassie and Rin Tin Tin—are not the only pet heros and heroines. For instance, there is Lucky, a black tomcat owned by Mrs. Dorothy Kennedy of Abbots Morton, England.

In February 1981, Kennedy, a 67-year-old widow, was postmistress of the local British post office. On her way to work one day, she was accosted by a thug who demanded all her money and possessions. Mrs. Kennedy was about to co-operate when suddenly her black tomcat Lucky, evidently aware of what was happening, attacked the robber by jumping on his back and clawing him. The robber, amazed at the audacity and ferocity of the cat, quickly forgot about Mrs. Kennedy and her money and fled the scene in shock and fright. The unharmed Mrs. Kennedy had Lucky to thank for rescuing her from the clutches of the would-be robber.

After her story was corroborated by witnesses, the post office awarded Lucky a certificate for "bravery and loyalty." It was the first time the conservative British postal office had ever so honored an animal, and *a cat* was the official hero!

Lucky was a heroic cat who rescued his mistress from the clutches of would-be muggers.

Lucky's story, however, does not end on a happy note. The following October Lucky was killed by a car just outside the post office where he had once proven his bravery and quick-thinking ability. Heartbroken, Mrs. Kennedy said that her only consolation was that he appeared to have died instantly.

To name your pet after a hero or heroine would be a wonderful thing to do, but one word of caution about using this category may be in order. While it may appear a kind act of remembrance to name a pet after a hero, or exciting to use the name of a famous movie, television, or other type of celebrity, keep in mind the effect and the expectations placed on your pet. First, heed the words of Voltaire who said in 1723, "It is a heavy burden to bear a name that is too famous."

After Pets of Famous People

Famous people are of course just human and so they naturally have beloved pets. Indeed, the most famous (and infamous) of folks have pets. And, these pets all have names which you can adopt for your own pet. Our list includes a substantial number of these names of pets owned by stars ranging from Dolly Parton to Zsa Zsa Gabor.

Perhaps the most interesting names, and the most entertaining and usable, are those of pets owned or once owned by the presidents of the United States and their immediate families. We have devoted an entire section to these intriguing pet names.

Extensive research has enabled us to record the names of pets of every president, from George Washington to Ronald Reagan. Perhaps the list does not include *every* pet *ever* owned by a president, but we guarantee you will not be able to find any list of presidential pets more comprehensive than the one in this book.

It is fascinating to scan this list (see Section I in Chapter 5) and delight in the names given presidential pets. It causes one to conjure up exciting visions of General George Washington accepting the British surrender at Yorkstown (1781) while sitting on his favorite horse, Nelson, or Franklin Roosevelt with his faithful Scotch terrier, Fala, by his side at important World War II conferences. In modern times, we can have fun envisioning President Ronald Reagan roughhousing with his husky, Taca or Amy Carter (daughter of President Jimmy Carter) playing merrily with her cat, Misty Malarky Ying Yang.

To Match Profession of Owner

One of the most delightful and innovative methods to use in selecting that "just right" moniker is to choose a name that matches the profession of the owner. For example, J. Edgar Hoover, the late director of the FBI, named his dog G-Boy; pianist Liberace gave his poodle the fitting appellation of Minuet; and General George Marshall, a strong advocate of a Western military alliance, picked the appropriate name NATO for his canine.

The name you choose would be one that seems to perfectly correspond with an attribute of your profession. For example:

For the Profession of	How About
Vehicle Mechanic	Tune-up
Soldier	Stripes
Hair Dresser	Cutter
Minister	Amen
Computer Analyst	Hi-Tech
Athlete	Umpire (or Ump)
Gas Station Attendant	Fill'r Up
Secretary	Typo
Waitress	Tips
Trucker	Wheels
Banker, Cashier, Teller	Bux
Gambler	Roulette
Dancer	Kicker
Doctor	Say-Ahh!
Attorney	Your Honor

Names with Special Meaning

A delightful way to name pets is to choose a name with a very special meaning. The English language abounds with terms and words derived from Hebrew, Greek, Latin, and Teutonic tongues which, history reveals, had original meanings of special and often pleasant significance. For instance, note the following:

> Richmond (originally meant Mighty Protector)
> Adlar (noble and brave)
> Adonis (handsome)
> Sacha (helper of mankind)

Some pet parents prefer a name with special meaning, feeling that it denotes a special aura of depth to the pet's relationships with humans. Therefore, we do include quite a few names of this category in our listing. These include both names from earlier eras and modern times.

There is, however, a problem that may arise by using such a name. This might occur if the original meaning for the name is so ancient or otherwise obscure that people, upon hearing it, misinterpret its meaning. Take a name like Rowena which, in Celtic, meant "white mane." Also, Rowena was the heroine of the novel *Ivanhoe* (1819) by Sir Walter Scott. A very romantic name, for sure. However, if you name your pet Rowena, expect to be bombarded with questions by strangers, curious to know why you chose such an unusual name. Of course, if you enjoy light conversation and draw entertainment from it, this might be an advantage and not a hindrance.

Another piece of cautionary advice: if you use a *contemporary* term, be sure the meaning is one commonly held. One woman told us that she had named her cat Coke. "Because she's 'the real thing'," she exclaimed with pride. However, she confided to us that sometimes she regrets the choice, because it is so often misunderstood. Surprisingly, some people comment how Coke the cat does not look at all like a Coke bottle. A few have asked the woman if she was into drugs—the term "coke" is a short version of cocaine.

For Special Reasons

Finally, there are names selected for reasons unique to the owners of a pet. For instance, a single gentleman of our acquaintance takes his dog, Hotlegs, out for a walk each day in a scenic city park. He finds that single young women are greatly attracted to a man walking a pet! For one thing, the pet gives the young ladies a reason to stop and initiate a conversation. The first thing they ask is, "What is your cute dog's name?" When he responds with, "Hotlegs," they usually burst into laughter. Invariably, they plead with him to relate the story of how Hotlegs was tagged with that name. (Note: Our friend refuses to tell Wanda and me the story, jokingly promising he will tell it to Wanda *after* she and I get a divorce!)

Quite a few pet parents pick a name to commemorate their hometown, or a city, state, or area of the country they admire. The following names come to mind:

Austin	Miami
Jersey	Big Apple (for New York)
Detroit	

Occasionally, the given name or surname of a *person* is adopted for a pet. Thus, our list includes such names as:

Smith	Loretta
Robert	Jimmy
Mary	Jake

This could be a problem—albeit a humorous one.

An interesting episode in the life of President Theodore Roosevelt occurred when his children's pet guinea pig was giving birth to little baby piglets. The mother guinea pig's name was Father O'Grady, the result of a friendly and amusing gesture made to a family priest of the same name.

As the president was busy in the Oval Office greeting dignitaries, the children rushed in unexpectedly. "Daddy, Daddy," they cried out excitedly. "Father O'Grady just had babies!"

Wouldn't it have been fun to be there and see the looks on the faces of the distinguished visitors?

Another special reason to tag a particular name on a pet is when the circumstances just seem to call for it. A man in Neptune, New Jersey, named his German shepherd Old Glory because of an unusual occurrence. Old Glory was kept in the fenced backyard where there was also a flagpole. The owner of the dog was a patriotic gentleman who each morning at exactly the same hour unfurled and raised the U.S. flag on the flagpole. Then, each evening just before dusk, he would lower the flag, fold and store it.

One morning, the German shepherd, wanting to be of assistance, rushed to the flagpole just as the flag was affixed to the cord on the pole. Grabbing the cord between his teeth, the canine gently but firmly pulled until the flag reached the top. This surprised his master. But that afternoon he had an even greater surprise. When he came to take down the stars and stripes, there was the faithful canine, insisting he be given the honor of bringing the red, white, and blue down. Every day thereafter, the German shepherd dutifully raised and lowered the flag. So naturally, the name Old Glory seemed appropriate and the dog was soon designated with the new appellation.

Cat lovers and fanciers need not fret that dogs are the only patriotic creatures. Margaret Graham of London, England, will attest that felines are just as loyal in allegiance to their country as Old Glory, the German shepherd.

According to a story in the London *Sunday Express,* Mrs. Graham's cats can properly be called the pride of the British Empire. It seems that Mrs. Graham simply could not get her finicky felines to answer her calls to dinner. No matter what she tried, the cats just did their own thing. This is, of course, quite normal behavior for the imperious and independent cat. Still, Mrs. Graham was frustrated at the cats' indifference to her pleas to come to dinner.

One evening, she tapped out the rhythm of "God Save the Queen" on their food dishes. Whoosh! They came running! The amused Mrs. Graham tested this method again and says it worked every time. This leads one to wonder if perhaps

Americans could get Morris the Cat (of Nine Lives cat food fame) to drop his finicky eater attitude at the playing of "Hail to the Chief" or the "Star Spangled Banner."

CHAPTER 4

MENTAL PREPARATIONS

Okay, so we know how to select a name that is "just so right" for both the pet and for you, the human parent. Now, let us get down to the mechanics. The first step you must take is to prepare yourself mentally. In fact, getting your mind honed and geared up is the most vital thing you can do in your search for an acceptable and exceptional name.

In this chapter we outline a method and some mental exercises to aid you in this search. If you are a person who is easy to please and the decision of selecting a name is not a difficult matter for you, great. It might be that you do not need the advice offered in this chapter. Not everyone does.

We know from experience that for many people the task of selecting a single name from among the thousands listed in this book is a bewildering and monumental task. For these people, probably a majority, a step-by-step name selection plan—such as we will describe here—is an invaluable, almost indispensable aid.

It certainly would have been a great aid for a friend of ours, a gentleman who had acquired a cute, little cocker spaniel puppy. Our friend, knowing we were writing this book, asked for and borrowed our preliminary list of the names. After pondering over all the many alternatives for days on end, unable to make a final decision, he finally gave up. The name he tagged on his new puppy: "Dog." "I went wild trying to make up my mind," he explained, "so I took the easy way out."

Obviously, not too original, right? But before faulting our friend, you may wish to consider that none other than Abraham Lincoln called his boyhood pet pig, merely, Pig and his pet dog, Fido. Later, as president, Lincoln's pet goat was christened by the ordinary pseudonym of Nanny.

Abe Lincoln's boyhood pet was a pig which he often rode like a horse.

One would think that a man like Lincoln, considered a literary genius for his masterpiece *The Gettysburg Address,* would be a bit more creative in picking names for his pets. But then, consider Lyndon B. Johnson.

President Johnson and his wife, Ladybird (now *that's* an original name for a *human* lady!), bequeathed the simple names Him and Her on their two pet beagles. Maybe genius sometimes lies in simplicity.

Notwithstanding the fact that there is some historical support in favor of simplicity, we are sure that few of this book's readers wish to name their canine simply "Dog," or their feline "Kitty" or "Cat." So . . . on to the task of choosing the *best* name possible.

PUTTING YOUR SUBCONSCIOUS TO WORK

The key to selecting a name is to let your subconscious mind perform at its peak. To accomplish this, it is important that you not attempt to select a name all at once. Do not, for example, sit down and expect to come up with a great name in just a few minutes or even a few hours. Instead, put your subconscious to work on this task several weeks before a decision has to be made. If this is not possible, then at least give your subconscious as much time as you can.

The subconscious is a wonderful thing, and, directed to complete a mental "to do" task, it very calmly and deliberately sets to work on the project. The subconscious works best when you *tell* it what you want it to do; that is, instruct it to consider and evaluate an appropriate name for your pet.

Initially, you should go over the list of possible names in this book (see Chapter 5). Silently read each and entrust it to your subconscious. Then, forget about it for approximately two weeks. Go about your normal day-to-day routine, with no conscious mental thought at all directed toward the task of selecting a name. Trust in the fact that while you tend to other things your subconscious is at work sifting through the names you have provided it, carefully evaluating the acceptability of each name, rejecting most, but culling those few, perhaps several, names which remain in prime contention as the finalists.

THE FINALS

After a few weeks of this subconscious mental preparation, it will be time to make the final name choice. This is the most important and crucial period, so plan to devote enough time to this task. Find a quiet place where you will not be disturbed and where there will be few mental distractions. Your mental reasoning functions best when the hub-bub of daily activity is put aside for a spell.

You should be alone during this period unless the name choice is to be the joint responsibility of a couple or an entire family, in which case the others involved should be present. It is important to be alone during this period and not to be encumbered with friends or other family members to whom the naming of the pet is of minor importance and who might therefore cloud up the process. Trust yourself. You will make a good choice of names because *you* have decided which name is best, not because a friend or acquaintance thinks another name might be better. You should be the sole judge.

Next, turn to the pages in this book listing the many names suggested for pets. The listing is conveniently divided into several categories.

A LIST OF FINALISTS

Your next step should be to prepare a list of potential names. Using the list in this book, go over each name, testing it mentally for appropriateness and fit. If necessary, say the name out loud, judging how it sounds when verbalized. It would be helpful if, during this procedure, you had the pet to be named present. In this case, while eyeing your pet, mentally picture yourself calling your pet by each possible name, and also picture how he might respond. If your pet cannot be present, then mentally visualize him—his personality and physical presence—as you consider each potential name, going through the same mental process described above. Discard those names which obviously do not "fit" or are in some way defective. On the other hand, write down each name that might be a "winner" on a sheet of lined notebook paper. Do not bother to prioritize your choices or to make a final selection at this time. That will come next.

When your preliminary list is finished, sit back and ask yourself if there are any other names not suggested in these pages which might be suitable. Write these names down as well.

AND THE WINNER IS . . .

Now you have your preliminary list drawn up. The next order of business is to prune this list to all but a few names. You should have at least half a dozen names on your preliminary list. Some persons may have as many as twenty-five; others might have been pleased with only a few. However, it is generally best to have a large number of possibles on the list, say, at least ten. So if your list is meager, you might wish to reconsider some of the names you rejected.

Regardless of the number of names on your final list, your job now is to narrow down your choices to only two or three. Use the following procedure to do this: write the number one, two, or three beside each name on your list. Number one represents the names you feel are most perfect, number two the names less perfect, and number three for those that are even less fitting.

Now, draw a line through to eliminate those in category number three. Then, perform the same procedure once again, assigning a one, two, or three to the remaining names, and casting out those in category number three. You should be left now with only a few names. It is possible you now have only *one* name remaining, in which case your job is over and your pet has a calling card to fit his and your tastes and life-style. Most people, however, will have at least two and possibly three or four names left on their list.

We now can proceed to the final selection of the "one best" name. Sit back, relax, and concentrate on the few names remaining. Evaluate each one in turn, restricting any thoughts on the other remaining alternatives. Go through the same process of mental visualization described earlier. Now, however, you are prepared to add two more criteria.

When considering each name, ask yourself, first, if you feel totally comfortable with the name; second, does saying the name aloud give you pleasant feelings and a sense of completeness. Judging the names, using these two criteria in conjunction with the mental (and/or physical) visualization of your pet's response to the name, will allow you to make a final selection: your pet's lifelong name.

THE POST-NAME SELECTION PERIOD

After you have made your choice, you should feel superbly thrilled and satisfied. Your lovely bundle of fur (or, perhaps, feathers) has a name—a beautiful name selected on the basis of the pet's and your unique personality and spirit.

Your friends and other family members will probably agree that the name is just perfect. Some, however, may protest that the name is not a good one. You will know better. And the new member of the family also will know better! Congratulations, Fido, Todd, Minnie, or . . . ?

CHAPTER 5

THE NAMES

Ready to tackle the names list? Be forewarned! Your task is a difficult one, for there are literally hundreds and hundreds of names suggested in this book. But it is also a satisfying task, especially in light of the end result.

We hope you have enjoyed the book. We are sure you are now fully prepared to evaluate the many names set forth here and winnow the possibilities down to one.

However, a few more words please before you begin. First, you may be interested in knowing how we were able to come up with such an extensive listing. Second, we need to tell you how we have categorized the broad list of names.

OUR SOURCES

The names in our list have been obtained from many different sources. We give our thanks and heartfelt appreciation to all those who helped us in our long quest for "the best" in pet names.

First and foremost there is our longtime friend, Nelda Stanley, who first suggested we write this book and who also gave us several ideas for names. Many other names were given to us by scores of people, pet-lovers whom we have met. A survey of selected veterinarians further aided us in composing our list. Then there were the hundreds and hundreds of biographies, novels, journals, newspaper and magazine articles, almanacs, and encyclopedias.

Many of our names were obtained from the files of Family Pets of America, a non-profit organization based in Austin, Texas. During our research, we also received a great deal of assistance from press secretaries, agents of movie and television stars, and personal secretaries of dignitaries, to whom we are grateful.

The final result of our great search for pet names amazes us. It especially should enlighten those with the mistaken belief that the number of pet names can be counted on one's fingers. Our research found an incredibly large number of names for pets, perhaps even exceeding the number of names given to humans. The assignment of names for pets, unlike those for people, is not limited by convention, fashion, and fad. Pet names can denote place or location, personality or physical attributes, proper names, whimsical fantasy, or any one of a number of options.

Obviously, there are many more names of which we are not aware. We do not claim that ours in an inclusive list—you would need volumes and volumes to accomplish this, if you could at all. Nevertheless, we are confident that our list will be of enormous benefit to the happy new parents of "children." For somewhere in our extensive list resides that one special name that awaits *your* pet.

REGISTERED NAMES

The reader should note that we do not include any information as to the formal and official names registered with the various breed registries. The American Kennel Club (AKC) has on its rolls the names of literally thousands and thousands of purebred dogs, as do the nine cat registration agencies that perform this service. But the names registered with the AKC are often not the names used by the average owner on a day-to-day basis.

One finds in the AKC registry such championship line pet names as Chester's Justin Tyme, Golden Heart Arctic Tax Digby, Oaktree's Iristocrat, and Royal Rock Touch of Brass. I defy the owners to use such formal names to summon the sweet dog to dinner and expect a proper response.

The fact that these names are often created for show purposes is obvious. The fact that the AKC will not register more than one pet with the same name is another reason for the lengthy, invariably unique, and often impractical official names of registered pets. This is not to demean the vital role of the dog and cat registries in maintaining purebred bloodlines. This is a well-known fact. And, of course, many of the names in our list *are* undoubtedly also duly recorded in registry files.

SECTIONS

The list of names is divided into five sections:

    I.   Presidential Family Pets
   II.   Celebrity Pets and Animals
  III.   Pets of Famous People
  IV.   Names with Special Meaning
   V.   Over 2,500 More Names!

Best of luck to you and your new pet. May both of you enjoy the new name for many delightful years to come.

Section I
PRESIDENTIAL FAMILY PETS

GEORGE WASHINGTON   **Took Office 1789**

Horses:
- Blueskin
- Chinkling
- Fatima
- Jolly
- Leonidas
- Magnolia
- Nelson, Revolutionary War mount
- Rozinante
- Sampson
- Steady
- Traveler

Hound Dogs:
- Captain
- Cloe
- Clover
- Forester
- Lady
- Mopsey
- Rover
- Taster
- Tipler
- Searcher
- Sweetlips
- Vulcan
- Zeach

Parrot: Polly

ANDREW JACKSON   **Took Office 1829**

Horses:
- Bolivia
- Emily
- Lady Nashville
- Sam Patches, wartime companion
- Truxton, champion race horse

Parrot: Poor Poll

WILLIAM HENRY HARRISON   Took Office **1841**

Cow: Suki, Durham cow

JOHN TYLER   Took Office **1841**

Horse: The General

ZACHARY TAYLOR   Took Office **1849**

Horse: Old Whitey, wartime companion

ABRAHAM LINCOLN   Took Office **1861**

Dogs: Fido, yellow/brown mongrel
                Jip

Goats: Nanny
                Nanko

Horse: Old Bob

Turkey: Jack

ULYSSES S. GRANT   Took Office **1869**

Dog: Faithful, Newfoundland

Horses: Billy Button, Shetland pony
                Butcher Boy
                Cincinattus
                Egypt
                Julia
                Jennie
                Mary
                Reb, Shetland pony
                St. Louis

JAMES GARFIELD   Took Office 1881

Horse: Kit, brown mare

BENJAMIN HARRISON   Took Office 1889

Goat: His Whiskers

THEODORE ROOSEVELT   Took Office 1901

Badger: Josiah

Cat: Tom Quarz

Dogs: Jack, Terrier
Manchu, Chinese cocker spaniel
Pete, bulldog
Sailor Boy, Chesapeake retriever
Skip, black mongrel

Guinea Pigs: Bishop Doan
Bob Evans
Dewey Junior
Dewey Senior
Father O'Grady

Snake: Emily Spinach, garter (green)

WILLIAM TAFT   Took Office 1909

Cow: Pauline, a Holstein

WOODROW WILSON   Took Office 1913

Sheep: Old Ike, a ram who chewed tobacco

WARREN HARDING   Took Office 1921

Dogs:
Caswell Laddie Boy, Airedale
Champion Tintern Tip Toe, Airedale
Laddie Buck, Airedale
Oh Boy, bulldog

CALVIN COOLIDGE   Took Office 1923

Birds:
Enoch, goose
Goldy, yellow bird
Nip (and Tuck, see below), green canary
Old Bill, thrush
Snowflake, white canary
Tuck, green canary

Bobcat:
Smokey

Cats:
Blacky
Tiger, gray striped

Dogs:
Bessie, yellow collie
Blackberry, black chow
Boston Beans, small bulldog
Diana, Shetland sheepdog
    Renamed: Calamity Jane
    Then Renamed: Jolly Jane
King Kole, black Belgian police dog
Mule Ears, brown collie
Oshkosh, white collie
Palo Alto, bird dog—renamed Rob Roy
Paul Pry, Airedale
Peter Pan, wirehaired terrier
Prudence Prim, white collie
Ruby Rough, brown collie
Tiny Tim, chow

Donkey:
Ebenezer

Raccoons: Horace
                 Rebecca

HERBERT HOOVER   Took Office 1929

Dogs: Big Ben, fox terrier
                 Eaglehurst Gillette, Irish setter
                 Glen, Scotch collie
                 King Tut, police dog
                 Pat, police dog
                 Patrick, wolfhound
                 Sonny, fox terrier
                 Weejie, elkhound
                 Yukon, Eskimo dog

FRANKLIN D. ROOSEVELT   Took Office 1933

Dogs: Blaze, large mastiff
                 Fala, Scotch terrier (nationally famous)
                 Major, German shepherd
                 Meggie, Scotch terrier
                 President, Great Dane
                 Tiny, English sheepdog
                 Winks, Llewellyn setter

HARRY TRUMAN   Took Office 1945

Dogs: Feller
                 Mike, Irish setter
                 Tandy (boyhood companion)

DWIGHT D. EISENHOWER   Took Office 1953

Dogs: Heidi, Weimaraner
                 Spunky, black Scotch terrier
                     (boyhood pet)
                 Telex, black Scotch terrier
                     (wartime companion)

JOHN F. KENNEDY   Took Office 1961

Birds:
Bluebelle, parakeet
Maybelle, parakeet
Robin, canary

Cat:
Tom Kitten

Dogs:
Blackie
Buddy (childhood pet)
Butterfly, mix
Charley, Welsh terrier
Clipper, German shepherd
Moe, Doberman pinscher
Pushinka, white Samoyed
    (given by Premier Krushchev, USSR)
Steaker, mix
White Tips, mix
Shannon, Irish cocker spaniel
Wolf, wolfhound

Hamsters:
Billy
Debbie

Horses:
Blackjack (favorite horse)
Leprechaun
Macaroni
Sarda
Tex

Rabbit:
Zsa Zsa

LYNDON B. JOHNSON   Took Office 1963

Dogs:
Blanco, white collie
Dumpling, beagle
Edgar, beagle
Freckles, beagle

Her, beagle
Him, beagle
Kim, beagle
Little Beagle, beagle
Little Chap, beagle
Rover, boyhood dog
Yuki, yellow/brown mongrel

RICHARD M. NIXON   Took Office **1969**

Dogs: Checkers, cocker spaniel
            King Timahoe, Irish setter
            Pasha, Yorkshire terrier
            Vicky, poodle

GERALD FORD   Took Office **1973**

Cat: Shan

Dogs: Liberty   (grandmother)
            Misty   (mother)
            Jackie   (grandchild)

            (Liberty, Misty, and Jackie are three
            generations of golden retrievers.)

JIMMY CARTER   Took Office **1977**

Cat: Misty Malarkey Ying Yang, mix

Dog: Grits, mongrel

RONALD REAGAN   Took Office **1981**

Dogs: Freebo
            Fuzzy, Belgian shepherd
            Lady, German shepherd

Millie, black Laborador retriever
Muffin, cockapoo
Taca, husky
Victory, golden retriever

Horses: Alamain, Arabian stallion
          (Gift from Mexico President,
          Lopez Portillo)
        Little Man
        No Strings
        Catalina
        Gwalianko

Ask any child to name five or six famous or celebrity pets and he can do it with ease. After that, though, it gets more difficult. Adults can remember considerably more names, but only an exceptional genius could recount the scores of names provided in this section.

Here are the "Four Star" pets and animals. Some, such as Bullet, Roy Rogers' famed movie horse, and Bonzo, the chimp (who once starred with Ronald Reagan in a movie), are living celebrities who gained fame through their own unique accomplishments. Others, like Black Beauty, a horse immortalized in a series of well-known books, are creations of authors, cartoonists, and poets. What is undeniable, however, is that *all* are celebrities.

Admiral	Champion horse
Agile	Won Kentucky Derby in 1905
Alsab	Race horse who won Preakness in 1942
Alpha	Dolphin from the movie *Day of the Dolphin*
Alpo	Mascot for Alpo Dog Foods
Alvin	Mischievous chipmunk in humorous hit records
Amber	Cat from the book *Amber a Very Personal Cat* by Gladys Taber
Arlecchino	Dog owned by Thomas Mann's daughter
Arnold	Pig star in TV series *Green Acres*
Assault	Famous thoroughbred horse; won Triple Crown in 1946
Asta	Dog star of '30s movie series *The Thin Man* with Myrna Loy and William Powell
Babar	Hero elephant of famed children's book
Babe	Blue ox owned by Paul Bunyan
Bambi	Beloved deer of Walt Disney movie fame
Banjo	Cartoon cat

Barko	Famous dachshund from Germany
Barnum	Famous race horse who won almost 300 races
Belka	Russian space dog
Benji	TV and movie star dog
Bigwig	Rabbit from the book *Watership Down* by Richard Adams
Blitzen	One of Santa's eight reindeer
Black Beauty	Horse immortalized in series of books
Bodidly	Hero dog cited by Humane Society
Boo	Name of dog from well-known country song
Boomer	Hero dog of TV series *Here's Boomer*
Bonzo	Famed actor-chimp who co-starred with President Ronald Reagan in movie *Bedtime for Bonzo*
Brighty	Burro in book *Brighty of the Grand Canyon* by Marguerite Henry
Buddy	First seeing eye dog in America
Bugs	Bunny rabbit character in comic strips
Bullet	German shepherd movie star; sidekick of Roy Rogers in western movies
Buttermilk	Movie star horse of Dale Evans
Champion	Movie star horse of famed cowboy Gene Autry
Chanticleer	Rooster in one of Chaucer's *Canterbury Tales*
Cheetah	Tarzan's movie chimp friend
Cheshire	A cat with a huge grin described in *Alice in Wonderland*
Chi Chi	The London Zoo's giant panda
Chips	Dog who was awarded the Distinguished Service Cross
Citation	One of most famous race horses in all history
Clyde Jr.	Orangutan movie star; co-starred with Bo Derek in *Tarzan the Ape Man* and with Clint Eastwood in *Any Which Way You Can*

Clarence	Lion in TV series *Daktari* set in Africa
Cleo	Basset hound from George Burns/Gracie Allen TV comedy series
Cock Robin	Bird in nursery rhymes
Cotton Tail	Rabbit from story of *Peter Rabbit*
Cupid	One of Santa's eight reindeer
Curly	Heroic dog cited by the Humane Society
Daffy	Walt Disney's lovable duck
Daisy	Dog in the comic strip *Blondie*
Dancer	Once again, one of Santa's reindeer
Dasher	Yet another of Santa's eight reindeer
DC	Siamese cat in movie *That Darn Cat*
Dingaling	Brave heroic dog who won Humane Society's award
Dinky	First Lhasa apso to become an American citizen
Donder	Another of Santa's reindeer
Dox	Police dog in Italy who captured hundreds of criminals
Dumbo	Flying baby elephant in movies
Eeyore	Donkey from comic strip *Winnie the Pooh*
Elmer	Bull mascot of Borden's Milk Company
Flame	Movie horse of Zane Grey's westerns in the '20s
Flicka	Horse in book *My Friend Flicka* by Mary O'Hara
Flipper	Dolphin movie star of TV and movies
Fozzie	Bear from *The Muppet Show*
Francis	Talking mule actor
Fred	Baretta's cockatoo in TV detective series
Fury	Black stallion star of many movies and TV
Gallant Man	Race horse; won Belmont Stakes in 1957
Garfield	Comic strip cat
Goofy	Walt Disney cartoon dog
Greyfriar's Bobby	Skye terrier dog famed for his loyalty
Grimalkin	Cat from Shakespeare's *MacBeth*
Harvey	Imaginary rabbit in TV specials
Henny-Penny	Hen of *Sky is Falling* children's story
Hsing Hsing	Giant panda in Washington Zoo

Hub	Boston terrier loved by President Harding; when Hub was poisoned the president wrote an impassioned newspaper editorial
Jackie	MGM lion renowned for his growl in the monogram prelude to movies
Jiminy	Cartoon cricket
Jock	Dog from Walt Disney movie *Lady and the Tramp*
Joe Young	Movie gorilla, distant cousin of King Kong
Judy	Chimp from the TV series *Daktari*
Kalamazoo	Name of cat from well-known country song
King Kong	Legendary giant ape of movie fame
Kittiwynk	Horse in the book *The Maltese Cat* by Kipling
Krypto	Superman's superdog
Lamb Chop	Well-known ventriloquist Shari Lewis' puppet lamb
Laika	Very famous Soviet space dog; was first animal to orbit the earth
Lassie	Mammoth collie movie star of TV and movie fame
Leo	Lion from the MGM trademark
Major	Lion hero in Walt Disney's book and movie *Napoleon and Samantha*
Mama Cat	Artist Kliban's cat
Man O' War	Famous race horse
Messenger	Beloved horse buried in 1808 with full military honors
Mexique	Mule that served in the Army for some 40 years and commended by General Sherman in a letter to the Secretary of War
Mickey Mouse	Walt Disney's famed cartoon character
Minnie Mouse	Feminine friend of Mickey Mouse
Mighty Mouse	Walt Disney's super mouse
Miss Piggy	Beauteous and feminine pig, star of the *Muppet Show*
Misty	Famous movie performer horse; made 70 movies in the 1920s and 1930s

72

Moby Dick	The killer whale in the classic book by Herman Melville
Moon	Dog cited for heroism by Humane Society
Morris	Famous TV model for Nine Lives Cat Food commercial
Muska	Shot into space by Russians in early space mission
Mr. Ed	Horse who won awards for his role in TV series
Nashua	Famed racehorse
Needles	1956 Kentucky Derby winner
Nessie	The Loch Ness monster
Nipper	The dog trademark symbol of RCA; "His Master's Voice"
Odie	Abused dog from Garfield cartoons
Omaha	Triple Crown winner racehorse
Peng	Incredible dog who served as a co-pilot in the Israeli Air Force
Peter	Rabbit from *The Tales of Peter Rabbit*
Phoenix	The Phoenix bird, according to mythology, lived up to 1,000 years. After burning to ashes it is said the Phoenix magically arose to live again
Pluto	Walt Disney's cartoon character
Pogo	Opossum in cartoon by Walt Kelly
Porky	Stuttering pig of cartoon renown
Pooch	Dog who won Humane Society's award for bravery
Prancer	One of Santa's reindeer
Pyewacket	Siamese cat from movie *Bell, Book and Candle*
Rin Tin Tin	Famous 1930s star German shepherd
Rivets	Comic strip dog
Rudolph	The red-nosed reindeer from Christmas legend
Ruff	Dog in comic strip *Dennis the Menace*
Sahi	Porcupine in *The Jungle Book* by Kipling
Sandy	Broadway star dog in *Annie*; portrayed dog belonging to Little Orphan Annie

Scout	Tonto's horse from *Lone Ranger* series
Secretariat	Triple Crown winner race horse
Sharpie	Parrot in Gillette TV commercials
Shep	Faithful and heroic dog in American song and folklore
Silver	The Lone Ranger's famed white horse
Smoky the Bear	Forest fire prevention symbol
Snoopy	Long-eared beagle from Charlie Brown comic strip *Peanuts*
Spark Plug	Comic strip racehorse
Spithead	Sir Isaac Newton's journal mentioned this cat
Spot	Lovable dog in millions of American first grade reading books
Strelka	Russia's space dog that orbited in space
Sugah	Pet goat awarded $115,000 in will
Teddy	Name became universally popular when President Theodore Roosevelt caught a baby bear. Newspaper cartoon captioned "Teddy's bear" caught the public's fancy and the rage for teddy bears was on
Tige	Buster Brown's dog who "lives in a shoe"
Tony	Horse star ridden by western cowboy star Tom Mix
Toto	Dorothy's lovable mutt in *The Wizard of Oz*
Tramp	Dog from movie *Lady and the Tramp*
Trep	World acclaimed drug-sniffing police dog
Trigger	Trusty steed of Roy Rogers
Tweety	Animated cartoon bird
Vanilla	Famous gorilla housed in Houston Zoo
Vixen	Another of the eight reindeer who pulled Santa's sleigh
Wei Wei	Giant panda performer
Whichone	Highly acclaimed champion race horse
Whirlaway	Thoroughbred horse who won Triple Crown
White Fang	White wolf-like dog from Jack London novel

Woodstock	Canary in *Peanuts* comic strip
Woody	Owl in TV commercials who asks people to "Give a Hoot, Don't Pollute"
Yogi	Bear in children's cartoon series
Zev	Kentucky Derby winner

"There must be a mistake. My name's Rover."

Names in this section are divided into five parts:

(1) Pets of television and movie stars and personalities

(2) Pets of literary artists (poets, authors, historians, play-wrights)

(3) Pets of political and military leaders (historical and modern-day)

(4) Pets of other famous people

PETS OF TELEVISION AND MOVIE STARS
AND PERSONALITIES

Luci Arnaz
    Dog: Wickle

Catherine Bach
    Cat: Kitty, white chinchilla Persian

Betty Barrett
    Cat: Pepper, Persian

Sarah Bernhardt
    Dog: Hamlet

Amanda Blake
    Lion: Kemo

Erma Bombeck
    Dogs: Arlo, Irish setter
                Jessamyn, poodle

Pat Boone
Dog: Frosty, poodle

Quinn Cummings
Dog: Ginger
Calico cat: Pooh

Doris Day
Dogs: Biggest
                  Bobo
                  Bubbles
                  Charlie
                  Muffy, poodle
                  Schatzie, dachshund
                  Tiny

Phil Donahue
Dog: Tida, Maltese terrier

Donna Drake
Rabbit: Fasadini

Sandy Duncan
Dog: Charlie, white terrier

Katherine Cornell
Dog: Fluff

Johnny Crawford
Horse: Two Bits

Totie Fields
Dog: Bubbles

Errol Flynn
Cat: Bes Mudi, Siamese

Eva Gabor
Dogs: Baby, Yorkshire terrier
                  Googie, Yorkshire terrier
                  Kis Lany, German shepherd

Janet Gaynor
    Dog: Missy
    Cat: Super Cat

Dorothy Gish
    Dog: Rover, Pekingese

Lorne Greene
    Dogs: Ginger
              King

Robert Goulet
    Dog: Lance, German shepherd

Merle Haggard
    Dogs: Wawe, toy terrier
              Pepper, toy terrier

Rex Harrison
    Dogs: Homer, basset hound
              Jason, basset hound
              Tara, basset hound

Charlton Heston
    Dog: Drago, German shepherd

Janet Leigh
    Cat: Turkey

Jerry Lewis
    Dog: Angel, poodle

Liberace
    Dog: Minuet, poodle

James and Pamela Mason
    Cats: Anna, Siamese
              Angus Silky, Siamese
              Baby
              Folly, Siamese
              Gamma, Siamese
              Tree

Dogs: Cheo
                    Skipper

Olivia Newton John
    Cat: Gypsy
    Dogs: Domino, Great Dane
                    Zargon, Great Dane

Hugh O'Brian
    Dog: Panda

Donny and Marie Osmond
    Dog: Fuji, Akita dog owned in childhood

Jack Parr
    Lion: Amani

Dolly Parton
    Dogs: Lickety Spitz, spitz
                    Mark Spitz, spitz

Jane Pauley
    Cat: Meatball

Robert Reed
    Dog: Mister Stubbs

Susan St. James
    Dog: Kiddo

Suzanne Somers
    Goldfish: Bif
                    Muffy

Sally Struthers
    Cats: Baba
                    Scooty

Elizabeth Taylor
    Chipmunk: Nibbles
    Dogs: Elsa, Lhasa apso
                   Reggie, Lhasa apso

Ellen Terry
    Dog: Fussy

Arthur Treacher
    Dog: Belle, Yorkshire terrier

Rudy Vallee
    Dog: Mony

Gwen Verdon
    Cats: Fatrick
                   Feets Fossee
                   Tidbits

John Wayne
    Dog: Duke, Airedale (boyhood companion)

Natalie Wood
    Cat: Jaws
    Dog: Centime

PETS OF LITERARY ARTISTS

Matthew Arnold
    Cat: Toss, Persian

Noel Behn
    Cat: Noname

Elizabeth Barrett Browning
    Dogs: Faunus
                   Flush, spaniel

Lord Byron
    Dog: Boatswain, Newfoundland

Thomas Carlisle
    Cat: Columbine, black

Raymond Chandler
    Cat: Taki, Persian

Alexander Dumas
    Bird: Jurgatha, vulture
    Cat: Mysouff

Edward Lear
    Cat: Foss

Alexander Pope
    Dog: Bounce, Great Dane

Sir Walter Scott
    Cat: Hinse

John Steinbeck
    Dog: Charley, poodle

James Thurber
    Dogs: Christabel, poodle
                 Jennie

Mark Twain
    Cats: Appollinaris
                 Beelzebub
                 Blatherskite, Siamese
                 Sour Mash
                 Zoroaster

PETS OF POLITICAL AND MILITARY LEADERS

Alexander the Great (Greek conqueror)
    Horse: Bucephalus

Omar Bradley (5 star general, World War II)
    Dog: Beau, poodle

Hernando Cortez (Spanish conquistador)
    Horse: El Morzillo

General George Custer (U.S. Army)
    Horse: Vic

Thomas Dewey (governor of New York)
    Dog: Canute

Duke of Wellington (British general; defeated Napoleon)
    Horse: Copenhagen

Barry Goldwater (U.S. Senator)
    Dog: Cyclone
    Mule: Sunny, campaign mascot

Adolph Hitler (German Nazi leader)
    Dog: Blondi, Alsatian

J. Edgar Hoover (FBI chief)
    Dogs: Cindy, Cairn terrier
                 G-Boy, Cairn terrier

Hubert H. Humphrey (Vice President, U.S.A.)
    Dog: Doc, hunting dog

Robert F. Kennedy (U.S. senator)
    Dog: Freckles
    Guinea Pig: Crooked Coconut
    Salamander: Shadrack

Robert E. Lee (Civil War general)
    Horse: Traveler

Louis IX (King of France)
    Dog: Bleu

George C. Marshall (U.S. Army general, presidential adviser)
Dogs: Bones
                  Nato

Mohammed (prophet, founder of Moslem religion)
Camel: Al Kaswa, his favorite
Cat: Muezza, white cat

Daniel P. Moynihan (U.S. senator)
Dog: Whiskey, terrier

Couve de Murville (French diplomat)
Dog: Xenophon, dachshund

Napoleon (Emperor of France)
Horse: Jaffa

Thomas Paine (Revolutionary War hero)
Horse: Button

John Pershing (general, commander of Allied Forces,
World War I)
Horse: Kidron

Rameses II (Pharaoh of Egypt)
Lion: Anta-M-Nekht

Victoria I (Queen of England)
Cat: White Heather
Dogs: Marco, Pomeranian, the Queen's favorite
                  Turi, poodle

Harold Wilson (British prime minister)
Dog: Paddy, Laborador retriever

PETS OF OTHER FAMOUS PEOPLE

Clyde Beatty (circus magnate)
Dog: Lucky

Lucius Beebe (journalist)
Dog: T-Bone, St. Bernard

Buffalo Bill (Wild West showman)
Horse: Steamboat, showhorse

Daniel Boone (pioneer frontiersman)
Cat: Bluegrass

George Booth (cartoonist)
Cat: Savortooth

Richard Byrd (admiral, Arctic explorer)
Dog: Igloo, mongrel who accompanied Admiral
Byrd in 1928 on expedition to South Pole

Eileen Ford (owner, fashion model agency)
Cat: Kiki

Patty Hearst (kidnapped heiress)
Dog: Arrow

Robert Indiana (artist)
Cat: Petepeetoo

Louis B. Mayer (movie czar)
Horse: Alibhai, Thoroughbred

Glen Miller ('40s band leader)
Dog: Pops

Sir Isaac Newton (scientist)
Dog: Diamond

Albert Schweitzer (African missionary, Nobel Prize winner)
Cat: Sizi

Gene Shalit (movie critic)
Cat: Junior

Liz Smith (syndicated columnist)
Cat: Mister Ships

Section IV
NAMES WITH SPECIAL MEANING

The following names were selected because of their histori-
cally significant definition. They derive from many sources,
especially the Greek, Teutonic, Hebrew, and Latin languages.
One may provide you with that special meaning so very
appropriate for your very own pet.

—A—

Abby	Joyful
Abra	Mother of multitudes
Abraham	(Abe) Father of multitudes
Acacia	Honors Saint Acacius, the "good angel" and protector of children
Achilles	Mythical hero of Homer's *Iliad*
Adam	Of the red earth
Adlar	Noble
Adonis	Youthful and beautiful
Adora	A gift
Adorabelle	Beautiful and admired
Ajax	Eagle; brave and strong
Alban	White, fair, or shining
Albert	Noble and brilliant
Alda	In good spirits
Alexa	Amiable
Aloha	Hawaiian for love, greetings, and farewell
Alric	Ruler
Alvin	Noble friend liked by all
Amber	A jewel of reddish-yellow color
Amos	Burdensome
Amy	Beloved
Angel(a)	Messenger from above
Ann	Grace
Apollo	Greek God, symbolizes male beauty and intelligence
April	Open and light, as in the spring season

Argus	To be vigilant and all-seeing
Arthur	In honor of the great King Arthur
Arvin	A friend
Asta	A star
Athena	In Greek mythology, the goddess of wisdom
Azura	Persian for sky-blue in color

—B—

Bangles	Decorative in nature
Begonia	Showy flower
Belinda	Lithe, elusive, and willowy
Bella	Beautiful
Beryl	Like a jewel
Bianco(a)	Fair and white
Biddy	Cheerful or gossipy
Blondie	Fair haired
Blossom	To come forth, as to bloom or flower
Blythe	To be happy or joyous
Bonita	Pretty
Bonus	An extra; more than expected
Bridget	The mighty or most high
Bubbles	Lively and rambunctious
Buttercup	Yellow and fresh

—C—

Cactus	Prickly and enduring
Caesar	Imperial, as in Julius Caesar
Calder	Stony or flowing
Calla	A flower; one of the most spectacular lillies
Calliope	Poetic and a beautiful voice
Calvin	The bald
Cameo	Special and distinctive
Candy	Candid, honest, and pure
Caprice	Humorous
Capricorn	Heavenly origin
Caramel	A sweet charmer
Casper	Persian word for treasure
Cass	Helpful
Catrina	Graceful and balanced

87

Celeste	Heavenly
Charity	Love or caress; grace
Chauncey	Chancellor; a high official
Chelsea	Comely and alluring
Cheri	French for sweetheart
Chris	Golden flower
Cinders	Ashes
Clarissa	Bright, fair and clear
Clementine	Merciful
Cleo	Famous
Clover	Sweet, as in the fragrant clover
Cocoa	Mellow and dark
Columbia	High-flying dove
Conchita	Saucy
Concordia	Old-fashioned
Cookie	Sweet and delectable
Coral	Protection
Cornelia	Lovely jewel
Crescent	To increase or create
Crispin	Curly haired
Crystal	Ice clear and transparent
Cupcake	Tiny, dainty, and lovable
Cupid	God of love
Cyclone	Whirlwind or storm
Cyrus	Persian for the sun; Cyrus the Great founded the Persian Empire

—D—

Daffodil	Yellow flower that blooms in the spring
Daffy	Silly or foolish
Dagmar	The glory of the Danes
Daisy	The day's eye; first class
Dale	Valley
Dallas	Playful or skilled
Dalton	A farm in the valley
Daphne	Greek meaning the laurel
Darcy	Dark or strong
Daria	Wealthy; queen
Dauphine	Royal

Dawn	Light in the morning
Delight	Pleasurable
Delilah	Delicate
Delta	The fourth; friendly
Desire	Longed for
Destiny	Fortunate arrival
Diamond	Shiny or sparkling
Dixie	From the South; the tenth
Dolly	Special; little girl; child sweetheart
Dora	Gift
Duchess	Aristocratic and noble
Ducky	Just fine
Dumpling	Favorite; just a little bit
Dusty	Powdery; tan color

—E—

Easter	Spring, dawn
Echo	Repetition of sound
Edris	Rich ruler
Effie	Famous
Electra	Flashy and bright
Elissa	Truth
Elmo	Friendly
Elvira	Fair
Embla	First female
Emerald	To glisten; green-eyed
Enid	Spotless
Erica	Regal
Esmeralda	Like a gem
Esther	The Star
Etna	Furious and explosive
Eva	Life
Evangeline	Bearer of good tidings

—F—

Fabia	Farms the earth
Faith	The virtue of trust
Fancy	Decorative add-ons
Fanny	Free and independent

Farrah	Exotic or exceptional
Fawn	Young
Feather	Light and airy
Felice	Joyous
Fidelia	Faithful and true
Fifi	Adding to one's life; fluffy and buoyant
Filly	Young and wild
Fiona	White and fair
Flavia	Blond; yellow-haired
Fleta	The fleet are swift
Flora	Flower
Florida	Healthy
Flossy	Beaming and luxuriant
Folly	Foolish; playful
Fortune	Chance
Freckles	Spotted
Friendly	Affectionate
Frisky	Playful; spunky
Fritz	Peaceful
Frosty	Cool
Fru-fru	Extra enjoyment
Frugal	Thrifty
Funnyface	Happy one

—G—

Gabby	Talkative
Gail (Gale)	Happy-go-lucky; devil-may-care attitude
Garland	Crowned for victory
Garnet	A radiant gem or stone
Gazelle	Graceful, quick and nimble
Gem	Precious jewel
Gemini	Twins
Gilda	Golden
Ginger	Spicy
Glamor	Beauteous; eyecatching
Glowworm	Glowing and luminous
Goldie	Precious
Grace	Loved, favored, honored
Granite	Hardy; stubborn

"Fifi refuses to go for any more drives unless we agree to put
her *name* on the license plate."

| Gretchen | Little divine pearl |
| Gypsy | Wanderer |

—H—

Hagar	Forsaken
Hale	Robust
Happy	Joyful
Harmony	Agreeable; in balance
Heather	Colorful; a violet flower
Hillary	Cheery and bright
Holly	Jovial
Honor	To hold in high esteem
Hope	To cherish
Hyacinth	Flower or jewel pertaining to the purple hyacinth flower

—I—

Ian	God's gracious gift
Ida	Rich or happy
Ilka	Each and every one
Imperial	Majestic or superior
Independence	Self-confidence; self reliant
Iodine	Red; antiseptic
Iris	The rainbow
Isadora	Moonstruck; fruitful
Ivan	Russian form of John
Ivy	Clinging

—J—

Jade	Green eyes or tint
Jam	Troublesome; sticky
Jama	Long and white; also daughter
January	To start or begin
Jasmine	Sweet fragrance
Jay	A bird; quick or lively
Jelly	Wobbly; sweet
Jemima	Patient; peaceful
Jessica	Long haired; independent
Jewel	Precious gem

Jezebel	Sinful
Jill(ian)	Little girl; flirt; sweetheart
Jingle	To make noise
Jocelyn	Jolly
Jordan	Descendant
Jove	Joy of life; fun
Joy	Filled with delight
Juliet	Romeo's sweetheart
June-bug	Bursting forth
Jynx (Jinx)	Bad luck; a spell or charm

—K—

Kama	Love
Karma	A mood of decisiveness; the way
Kasimir(a)	Command for peace
Katinka	Pure
Keira	Queenly
Kelda	A fountain or spring
Kent	White; bright
Kenyon	Blond haired; white
Kermit	God of arms
Kerry	Dark
Keven(in)	Loved; gentle
Keziah	Faithful
Kiki	Ornamental; helpful
Kinetta	Active
Kit	To accompany
Kittle	Cute behavior
Koko	Playful
Krinkle	Double measure

—L—

Lacy	Frilly
Lady	High class; upright female
Lady Bug	Best of Luck
Lala	Tulip
Lalita	Pleasing
Lancelot	One who serves; King Arthur's knight

Lanette	A little lane
Lang	Long or tall
Lani	Flower
Larissa	Cheerful
Lark	Carefree
Lasca	Weary
Lassie	Little Maid
Latham	Dweller by the barns
Leander	Courageous or lion-hearted
Leilani	Hawaiian for heavenly flower
Lenis	Smooth or soft-sounding
Leo	Courageous and strong
Leona	Feminine of Leo
Leslie	From the gray stronghold
Libby	Slightly overweight
Liberty	Free, true, steadfast
Lilah	Dark as night
Lionel	Lion-like
Livia	Frivolous
Lizzy	Consecrated by God
Lolita	A little lady
Lombard	Long beard
Lotus	Dreamlike state
Loverly	Affectionate
Lucky	Leading a charmed life
Lucy	Light
Lulu	Child born at dawn
Lydell	Wide open
Lydia	Voluptuous beauty

—M—

Mabel	Amiable
Mac	Prefix meaning "son of"
Madge	Pearl
Madison	Mighty in battle
Magnolia	Large and fragrant; "the great"
Magpie	Trickster
Mahrani	Princess
Mai-Tai	Tropical

94

Majestic	Stately
Malvin	Chief
Mansuette	Tamed, gentle one
Marigold	Gold flower
Marshall	One in charge of horses
Martibelle	Beautiful mistress
Marvelle	Wondrous
Max	The greatest
Mercer	Wheeler-dealer
Meredith	Protector from the sea
Merlin	Magician in King Arthur's court
Mignon	French for delicate or dainty
Mila	The lovable
Milca	Queen
Miles	The crusher
Millie	Independent; honey-sweet
Milo	Beautiful
Mimi	In Italian, "My! My!"
Minerva	Wisdom; force; mother
Minx	Insatiable
Miranda	Admirable
Missie	Little Miss
Mittens	Warmth
Mitzy	Purposeful
Modesty	Chaste; lack of arrogance
Molasses	Brown sugar
Monkey	Playful; agile
Moppet	Cute
Mousy	Shy and timid
Muffin	Delicious; edible
Muzzle	Restraint

—N—

Nada	Hope
Nappy	Restful and lazy
Natalie	Christmas child
Natasha	Russian form of Natalie
Nevada	Snowy
Nina	Little girl

Norval	Scottish sheep-tender
Nyx	Of the night

—O—

Oak	Hearty and durable
Octavi(us)	Eighth born
Odyssey	Journey
Oliver	Peace
Olympia	Heavenly
Omar	The better
Omega	Final or the last
Oneida	The awaited one
Opal	Precious one
Ophelia	Invincible and wise
Orchid	Majestic flower
Oscar	Leaping warrior
Otto	Prosperous or wealthy
Oui	Yes
Owen	Well-born
Ozora	Strength of the Lord

—P—

Page	Attendant or servant
Pamper	To spoil or indulge
Pandora	Gifted
Pansy	Thoughtful
Patience	Unhurried
Patrick	Noble
Paul	Little
Paxton	Traveler; trader
Peace	Without conflict
Pearl	Round-shaped beauty
Penney	Weaver
Pepita	"He shall add"
Perdita	The lost; in Shakespearean tales Perdita was the daughter of a king, raised to care for sheep
Perfecta	The perfect one
Perizada	Descendant from fallen angels

Pert	Saucy
Petunia	White or bluish-red in color
Philander	Lover of mankind
Philly	Brotherly love
Phineas	Brazen mouth
Phoebe	The bright
Plaxy	Active
Poppy	Red, white, or yellow flower
Portia	Pertaining to pigs
Prim	Reserved
Proctor	Manager
Prosper	To do well
Putnam	Dweller by the pond

—Q—

Quack	Charlatan
Queen(ie)	Leader
Quentin	The fifth born
Quin	The wise
Quincy	Owned by the fifth
Quitter	One who ceases before task is completed

—R—

Rachael	The lamb
Radinka	Playful
Raggedy	Unkempt; ungroomed
Ramon	Mighty protector
Randy	Housewolf or protector
Regan	Kingly
Regina	Queenly
Rex(ana)	Of royal grace; queen/king; strength
Riccadonna	Rich and hard lady
Ripley	The shouter
Rivets	To fasten
Robin Hood	English hero who stole from rich to give to poor
Rochell(a)	Little rock
Romeo	Lover
Romilda	Glorious battle maid

Roscoe	Swift horse
Ross	Horse
Rover	A wanderer; curious
Roy	King
Royal	Kingly
Royce	A king's son
Ruby	Jewel
Rufus	Red-haired
Russell	Fox-like
Ryan	Laughing

—S—

Sabra	To rest
Sacha	Defender of men
Saki	One who gives
Salome	Peace and welfare
Samantha	The listener
Sancia	The sanctioned one
Sapphira	Deep blue jewel
Scarlet	Deep, rich red
Sebastian(a)	The revered one; saintly
Shaggy	Tangled, unevenly cut
Sherry	The dry
Shoo Shoo	To overstay one's welcome
Silas	Of the forest
Siren	Loud or tempting
Sizzle	Hot or steaming
Slinky	Sneaky and hard to hold
Snooks	Good tempered
Snowy	White
Solon	Wisdom
Spanky	Fast and playful
Speedy	Swift
Squeaky	Noisy or clean
Stella	Top performer
Sterling	Genuine
Stormy	Temperamental
Suds	Energetic
Sugar	Sweet

Sunny	Optimistic
Sunshine	Bright and warm
Suzy-Q	Perfect charmer
Sweet Pea	Thin and nice
Swifty	Brisk

—T—

Tabasco	Hot and tart; spicy
Tabby	Swift; lunging
Taffy	Light in color
Taggard	Shaggy haired
Talbot	Bloodhound
Tally	Marker; score keeper
Tango	Fast moving
Terry	Tall like a tower
Thad	The praised
Theron	Hunter
Thumper	Weary and watchful
Tidbit	Small portion
Tiger	Aggressive
Toby	Goodness
Tom	Independent
Toner	One who sounds
Tony	Beyond praise
Topaz	Divine stone
Topsy	Light-hearted
Trevor	Prudent
Trinket	A small gift or souvenir
True	Fidelity or faithful
Truman	Faithful, loyal
Tubby	Big around the middle
Turtledove	Lovey; sweetheart
Twine	A twin
Tybalt	Bold for the people; a prince or leader
Tyrone	Lord

—U—

Ulf	German for wolf
Ulysses	Angry or wrathful; one who hates

Uno	"The one"
Urban	From the city
Uriel	Regent of the sun
Urien	From heaven
Uzziah	A mighty king

—V—

Valentine	Greeting; health
Valiant	Strong; powerful
Varian	Changeable; inconsistent
Vashti	Persian for the beautiful
Vaughn	The little
Vedette	The vigilant
Victor	Conqueror
Vincent	Conquering
Vito	The vital
Vladimir	Slavic or Russian for world ruler
Volley	More than one in succession

—W—

Wade	One who moves forward
Walden	Mighty
Waldo	One who rules or wields power
Wart	A bother
Weylin	Son of the wolf
Whistler	One who whistles
Whiz	Super smart
Willard	Determined
Winchester	Friendly
Winky	Bright and energetic
Winston	Firm friend

—X—

X	Mixed or unknown
Xanthe(ine)	The yellow-haired
Xavier	Bright
Xenia	Hospitable and friendly
Xenos	The stranger
Xerxes	Dictator
Xylon(a)	Of the wood

—Y—

Yale	One who gives in
Yancy	Of English ancestry
Yardley	From the garden
Yates	Gate guard
Yolanda	Strong
Yuma	A chief's son
Yvonne	Accurate

—Z—

Zadie	Princess
Zandra	Helper of mankind
Zenda	Womanly
Zeralda	Armored warrior maid
Zero	Empty
Zipper	Snappy and fast
Zippy	Lively
Zsa Zsa	Pretty and full of life

Section V
OVER 2,500 MORE NAMES!

If after earnestly reviewing the previous lists of pet names, you still have not found that perfect name for *your* pet, do not fret. On the following pages you will find over 2,500 more names for your consideration.

—A—
A.J.
Abbot
Abby
Abe
Abel
Abey
Abigail
Abner
Ace
Acey
Action
Ada
Addie
Adeine
Adel
Adela
Adelaida
Adele
Adena
Adlai
Adler
Adolph
Adolpho
Adria
Adriana
Adrienne
Ag
Agata

Agatha
Aggie
Agna
Agnella
Agneta
Agnola
Agosto
Agustin
Aila
Ailene
Alameda
Alanna
Alastair
Alberta
Albertina
Albie
Albon
Alcia
Alcina
Alden
Aldo
Aldon
Aldous
Aldus
Alex
Alexandria
Alexandrino
Alexina
Alexis

Alf
Alfi
Alfons
Alfonso
Alfreda
Ali
Alice
Alisha
Alissa
Alla
Allard
Allegra
Allegro
Allie
Allina
Allison
Allsun
Alma
Alonzo
Alphonse
Alta
Althea
Alvie
Alvina
Alvis
Alyssa
Amabel
Amadeo
Amanda

Amandis
Amara
Amargo
Amata
Amelia
Amelina
Amelinda
Ameline
Amelita
Amerigo
Amery
Amil
Amity
Amory
Anabelle
Anastasia
Anatola
Anatolia
Anders
Andie
Andrea
Andreanna
Ange
Angelica
Angelina
Angeline
Angelique
Angelita
Angelo
Angie
Angus
Anita
Annabelle
Annamarie
Annelise
Annette
Annie
Annora
Ansel

Anselmi
Anselmo
Anson
Anthony
Antoine
Antoinette
Antone
Antonetta
Antonia
Anya
Aprilette
Ara
Arabella
Archer
Attilla
Ava
Averil
Avis
Aviva
Aztec

—B—

B.J.
Babbie
Babbs
Babette
Bald
Baldin
Baldwin
Bali
Bambi
Banjo
Barbie
Bard
Barlie
Barnabus
Barnaby
Barney
Barrie

Bart
Bartie
Baruck
Bary
Basil
Bax
Baxie
Bayard
Bea
Bear
Beatrice
Beau
Beauregard
Bebe
Belita
Belle
Belva
Ben
Benedetta
Benedict
Benita
Bennie
Benton
Berk
Berkie
Bernadina
Bernadine
Bernard
Berni
Bernie
Bert
Bertha
Bertie
Bertram
Bess
Bessie
Beth
Betsy
Beulah

Bevan
Bevo
Bibb
Bibbs
Bibi
Big Bird
Bjorn
Black Bart
Blackjack
Black Sheep
Blankety Blank
Bo
Bo-Jangles
Bon Bon
Boone
Boonie
Boots
Bordie
Borg
Boris
Bossy
Bowie
Boy
Bradford
Brand
Brandy
Bren
Brenda
Brenna
Brett
Briana
Brianne
Bridgit
Bridid
Brita
Brittany
Bronnie
Bronson
Brooke

Broomtail
Brownie
Bruis
Bruno
Bud
Buddy
Bunny
Burgess
Burlie
Burr
Buster
Butch
Buttons
Buzz
Buzzsaw
Byron

—C—
Cadet
Caitlin
Cal
Calamity Jane
Calandra
Calandria
Calantha
Calico
Calida
Callie
Callista
Calypso
Cameron
Camille
Cammy
Camp
Campbell
Campy
Candace
Candice
Candida

Candie
Candra
Candy
Cara
Caresse
Cari
Carina
Carissa
Carla
Carleen
Carleton
Carlie
Carlin
Carlina
Carlita
Carlota
Carlotta
Carly
Carmel
Carmen
Carney
Carola
Carolina
Carrie
Carson
Carter
Carver
Casey
Cassandra
Cassidy
Cassie
Cassius
Catarina
Cate
Catha
Catie
Catriona
Caz
Cecie

Cecilius
Cele
Celesta
Celestia
Celia
Celie
Celina
Celinda
Celinka
Celka
Chad
Chaddie
Chaim
Chandra
Channing
Chap
Chappy
Charade
Charil
Charis
Charissa
Charita
Charity
Charla
Charline
Charlotta
Charmaine
Chastity
Chen
Cher
Cherice
Cherie
Cherry
Chesapeake
Chev
Chevis
Chevy
Chic
Chick

Chicka
Chloe
Chloris
Chopper
Chrisco
Chrissie
Christa
Christel
Christen
Christiana
Christie
Chrystal
Chuckles
Cicely
Cinderella
Cindy
Ciro
Cisco
Cissy
Clapper
Claresta
Clareta
Claretta
Clarette
Clari
Clarice
Clarie
Clarinda
Clarine
Claudette
Claudina
Claus
Clayborn
Clem
Clemence
Clementia
Clementina
Clemmie
Clemmy

Cleon
Clevie
Clint
Clio
Clip
Clive
Clyde
Cody
Colby
Colette
Colin
Collier
Commanche
Conan
Coney
Conlan
Connor
Conrad
Conrado
Constance
Constanta
Constantia
Constantine
Consuelo
Coop
Cooper
Cora
Corabel
Corabella
Corabelle
Coralie
Coraline
Corbie
Cordelia
Cordi
Corena
Corene
Coretta
Corey

Coriss
Corissa
Corliss
Cornelle
Cornie
Cory
Cosimo
Cosmo
Courtney
Creighton
Crisco
Crissy
Cristy
Critter
Crosby
Cross
Crow
Crown
Cullie
Curcio
Curran
Currey
Curt
Cy
Cyril
Cyrilla
Cyrillo
Cyrillus
Cynthia

—D—
Dace
Dacey
Daffie
Dahlia
Dal
Dalenna
Dalila
Dall

Damara
Damaris
Damian
Damita
Dan
Dana
Dane
Danette
Danielle
Danit
Danita
Danny
Dante
Danya
Dara
Darbie
Darby
Darcie
Dare
Dario
Darlene
Daron
Daryl
Davita
Deborah
Decca
Deck
Dee
Dee Dee
Deirdre
Del
Delia
Delinda
Della
Delly
Delmore
Delwin
Demeter
Demetra

Demetria
Demetris
Demp
Dempsey
Dena
Denby
Denise
Denison
Denny
Derby
Derry
Dersiree
Dervin
Dessau
Deva
Devlin
Devora
Dew
Dewie
DeWitt
Dex
Dexter
Di
Diana
Diane
Didi
Diego
Dieter
Dietrich
Dill
Dillie
Dillon
Dilly
Dimples
Dinah
Ding-a-ling
Dinky
Dinnie
Dinsmore

Dionne
Dionis
Dirk
Dizzie
Dmitri
Dodge
Dodie
Dody
Dog
Dolf
Dolfie
Dolores
Dolorita
Doloritas
Dolph
Dominic
Dominica
Dominico
Domino
Donahue
Donavan
Donella
Donna
Donni
Donny
Doralynn
Dore
Doreene
Dorelia
Dorella
Dorena
Dorene
Doretta
Dorette
Dorey
Doria
Dorice
Dorisa
Dorri

Dorry
Dos
Dossy
Dot
Dottie
Doubles
Drew
Druci
Drusie
Drusilla
Dud
Dudley
Duff
Duffy
Dukey
Duky
Dulcia
Dulciana
Dulcie
Dulcine
Dulcy
Dun
Dunce
Dustie
Dustin
Dwarf
Dyan
Dylan

—E—
Eartha
Eb
Eben
Ebenezer
Ebony
Eden
Edie
Edison
Ediva

Edmondo
Edna
Edrea
Edrena
Edsel
Edwina
Efrem
Egan
Egbert
Egon
Elana
Elayne
Elden
Eldridge
Eleanor
Eleanora
Eleazor
Elfreda
Eli
Elias
Elie
Elijah
Elisabetta
Elise
Elita
Eliza
Elizabet
Elizabeth
Ella
Ellen
Ellette
Elli
Elnora
Eloise
Elsa
Elsie
El Taco
Elton
Elvera

Elvina
Elvis
Elvyn
Elwin
Elwira
Elwood
Ely
Elyse
Elysia
Emerson
Emery
Emile
Emilio
Emlon
Emma
Emmaline
Emmie
Empress
Engelbert
Enrico
Ephraim
Eppie
Eraste
Erastus
Ericha
Erin
Erinna
Erma
Ermina
Erminie
Ernaline
Ernesta
Ernestine
Essa
Essie
Esta
Estella
Estelle
Estrella

Ethan
Etta
Ettie
Eugene
Eugenia
Eugenio
Eunice
Eustacia
Evan
Evangelia
Eve
Eveleen
Ewan
Ezekiel
Ezra

—F—
Fabian
Fabiano
Fabio
Fair
Fairfox
Fairley
Faline
Fania
Farrand
Farrel
Farris
Fauna
Fax
Fay
Fayette
Fayina
Felicia
Felicidad
Felicio
Felicity
Felita
Felix

Feliza
Felt
Felton
Felty
Fenton
Fenny
Ferd
Ferdie
Ferdinand
Fergus
Fern
Fernanda
Fernande
Fernandina
Fernando
Ferris
Fidel
Fidelity
Fidella
Fielding
Fifine
Filbert
Filberta
Filberto
Findley
Finn
Finnie
Fionnula
Fitz
Fitzgerald
Fletch
Fletcher
Flint
Flo
Florella
Floria
Florie
Floris
Florrie

"You can call me Day or you can call me Stray or you can call me Grey or Ray . . . but you doesn't has to call me Fido!"

Flossie
Fluff
Fluffpuff
Fluffy
Flyball
Fo
Focus
Fonz
Fonzie
Ford
Forest
Forevermore
Foss
Fossie
Foxy
Foxy Lady
Fran
Frances
Francie
Francine
Francisca
Francisco
Francoise
Frans
Frazer
Fred
Freda
Freddy
Fredella
Frederica
Frederoqie
Freida
Frenchie
Freya
Frieda
Fritzi
Fuzzy

—G—

Gab
Gabbie
Gabe
Gabriel
Gabriella
Galen
Galina
Gallager
Garner
Gasper
Gaston
Gay
Gene
Geneva
Genevieve
Gennie
Geoffrey
George
Georgeanne
Georgette
Georgia
Georgianna
Georgie
Georgina
Georgine
Gerald
Geralda
Geraldina
Geraldine
Gerard
Gerardo
Gerhardt
Germaine
Germana
Gerry
Gersham
Gert
Gertie

Gertruda
Gertrude
Gertrudis
Gerty
Gideon
Giffie
Gifford
Gigi
Gilbert
Gilberta
Gilbertina
Gilbertine
Giles
Gill
Gillie
Gilroy
Gina
Gino
Giovanni
Giraldo
Gisella
Giselle
Gladi
Gladys
Glenda
Glenine
Glennis
Glitter
Gloria
Gloriana
Gloriane
Glory
Glyn
Glynis
Golda
Goldarina
Goldia
Goldina
Go Go

Goodie-Two-
   Shoes
Governor
Gracia
Gracie
Grady
Granada
Granger
Granville
Grata
Gratia
Gratiana
Greer
Grete
Gretel
Gretta
Griff
Griffie
Griffin
Griffy
Griselda
Grissel
Grizel
Grizelda
Groovy
Grover
Guinevere
Gus
Gussie
Gustave
Gustavo
Gusto
Guthrie
Guy
Gwen
Gwendolyn
Gweneth
Gwenna
Gwennie

Gyp
Gypper

—H—
Hadley
Hal
Haldon
Halimeda
Hallie
Halona
Halsey
Hamil
Hamilton
Hamlet
Hamlin
Hana
Hanibal
Hank
Hankie
Hanna
Hanny
Hara
Haracourt
Hardy
Harlan
Harman
Harold
Harper
Harpo
Harri
Harrietta
Harriette
Harriot
Harrison
Hart
Harv
Harvey
Haskel
Hassle

Hastings
Hattie
Hazel
Hector
Hedda
Heddi
Heeby Jeeby
Heidi
Helen
Helenka
Helga
Helicopter
Helli
Heloise
Henri
Henrieta
Henrietta
Henriette
Herb
Herbert
Herbie
Hercule
Hercules
Herman
Hermie
Hermina
Hermine
Herminia
Hermione
Hermit
Hermosa
Hernando
Hersh
Hershel
Heshee
Hester
Hettie
Hewitt
Hilary

Hilda
Hildegarde
Hildy
Hillard
Hilly
Hilton
Hinda
Hippo
Hiram
Hobard
Hobby
Hobert
Hogan
Holbrook
Hollis
Holmes
Holt
Homer
Homing
Honda
Hondo
Honey
Honeybee
Honora
Horace
Horatio
Hortense
Horton
Hosea
Hoshi
Hotshot
Howie
Hubard
Hubert
Huberto
Hubie
Hugey
Hugh
Hughie

Hugibert
Hugo
Hulbert
Hum
Humbert
Humph
Humphrey
Hunt
Hunter
Huntington
Huntley
Hurdle
Hurley
Hussein
Hutt
Hutton
Hux
Huxley
Hyacintha
Hyacinthia
Hyacinthie
Hyatt
Hyman
Hymie

—I—
Iago
I Am
Idalia
Idalina
Idaline
Idelle
Idette
Ignace
Ignacio
Ignatius
Igor
Ike
Ilana

Ilene
Ilona
Ilonka
Ilsa
Imogene
Ina
Indy
Inez
Inga
Inge
Ingemar
Inglebart
Ingrid
Ingunna
Innis
Iola
Iona
Ione
Ira
Irene
Irena
Irisa
Irita
Irma
Irv
Irving
Irwin
Isa
Isaac
Isabeau
Isabelita
Isabella
Issi
Ivor
Izzie

—J—
J
JJ

Jacenta	Jayme	Jocky
Jacinda	Jean	Jody
Jacinta	Jeanette	Joe
Jacintha	Jeanie	Joel
Jack	Jeannette	Joella
Jackie	Jeannine	Joelle
Jacoba	Jemie	Joellen
Jacobina	Jenda	Johan
Jacobine	Jenica	Johannes
Jacqueline	Jeniece	John
Jacquenetta	Jennie	Johnny
Jacquenette	Jennifer	Jolene
Jacques	Jere	Jolie
Jacquetta	Jereme	Jonathan
Jacquette	Jeremiah	Jorge
Jaime	Jeremy	Josefina
Jaimie	Jerome	Josephine
Jakey	Jerrie	Josh
James	Jerry	Joshua
Jami	Jess	Josiah
Jamie	Jessalin	Josie
Jan	Jessalyn	Josselyn
Jana	Jessie	Joya
Janel	Jillana	Joyce
Janella	Jilli	Joypis
Janelle	Jilly	Jozef
Janet	Jim	Juan
Janeta	Jimminee	Juana
Janey	Jinks	Juanita
Jania	Jinny	Judah
Janice	Jo	Judd
Janine	Joachin	Jude
Janka	Joan	Jule
Janot	Joanna	Jules
Jany	Jobina	Juli
Jasisa	Joby	Julia
Jasmina	Jocelin	Juliana
Jason	Jock	Juliann
Jasper	Jocko	Julie

Julieta
Julietta
Juliette
Julina
Juline
Julita
June
Junette
Junia
Juniana
Junieta
Justin
Justina
Justino
Justus

—K—
Kacie
Kaiser
Kali
Kalika
Kalila
Kalinda
Kalindi
Kallie
Kama
Kamaria
Kameko
Kane
Karel
Karen
Karl
Karla
Karney
Kass
Kassia
Kassie
Kata
Katalin

Kate
Katerina
Katerine
Katey
Katha
Katharine
Kathie
Kathleen
Katina
Katrina
Katrinka
Katuscha
Katushka
Kay
Keely
Keenan
Keiko
Kelly
Kelsey
Kelso
Kendall
Kendra
Kenny
Kenton
Keriann
Kermie
Keuin
Khali
Killian
Killie
Kim
Kimberly
Kimbra
Kimmie
King Kong
Kinks
Kinky
Kinney
Kipp

Kippy
Kira
Kirby
Kirk
Kirsten
Kitty
Kleon
Kliment
Knox
Knute
Kodac
Kojac
Kora
Korene
Korie
Krista
Kristel
Kristen
Kristin
Kristina
Krysta
Kurt
Kyle

—L—
Lacey
Ladd
Laddie
Lady Di
Lainey
Laird
Lamar
Lambert
Lamberto
Lamonti
Lana
Lane
Laney
Lanny

Lara	Lenette	Lilias
Laraina	Lenny	Lilly
Larine	Lenore	Lilyan
Lasso	Leoine	Lina
Lathe	Leola	Lincoln
Lathrop	Leon	Linda
Latimer	Leonard	Lindi
Lattie	Leonelle	Lindsay
Laura	Leonie	Linette
Laure	Leonora	Link
Lauren	Leontine	Linnea
Laurena	Leopold	Linus
Lauretta	Leora	Lionello
Laurette	Leota	Lisa
Laurice	Leotie	Lisetta
Laurie	Leroy	Lisette
Laverna	Les	Lissie
Laverne	Lester	Liza
Lavina	Leta	Lizette
Lavinny	Letha	Lizzie
Lawford	Leticia	Llewellyn
Lawrence	Letisha	Lloyd
Lawton	Letizia	Lloydie
Lazare	Lettie	Loco
Lazarus	Lev	Logan
Leah	Levi	Logo
Leda	Levina	Lois
Lee	Lewie	Lola
Leeann	Lewis	Lona
Leanna	Lib	Lonnie
Leif	Libbie	Lora
Leigh	Lida	Lorelie
Leighton	Lil	Lorenzo
Leila	Lila	Lori
Leland	Lilas	Lorin
Lem	Lili	Lorna
Lemmy	Lilia	Lorrie
Lena	Lilian	Lotta
Lenci	Lilianna	Lottie

Lou
Louella
Louis
Louise
Love
Luana
Luann
Luanna
Luce
Lucia
Luciana
Lucie
Lucienne
Lucilla
Lucille
Lucina
Lucinda
Lucine
Lucita
Lucrece
Lucretia
Lucus
Ludie
Ludmilla
Ludovika
Ludwig
Luella
Luelle
Luke
Lulu
Luna
Lura
Lurette
Lurleen
Lurlette
Luz
Lydia
Lydie
Lyle

Lyman
Lynelle
Lynette
Lynn
Lyric
Lyrical

—M—
Mab
Mabella
Mace
Mackenzie
Mada
Madalyn
Maddie
Madel
Madelena
Madella
Madelle
Madie
Madlen
Mae
Magdala
Magdalena
Maggie
Magnur
Magoo
Mahala
Mahalia
Maida
Maisie
Major
Mal
Mala
Malachi
Malcolm
Malina
Mallory
Mamie

Mandel
Mandy
Manfred
Manuel
Manny
Mara
Marabel
Marcel
Marcella
Marcello
Marcellus
Marcia
Marcille
Marco
Maren
Margar
Margarette
Margarita
Marge
Margery
Margi
Margo
Margot
Maria
Marian
Marianna
Marianne
Maribel
Maribella
Marice
Maridel
Marie
Mariel
Marietta
Marilee
Marilyn
Marin
Marina
Mariquilla

Maris	Maxwell	Merrilee
Mariska	Maxy	Merrill
Marissa	May	Merry
Marista	Mayer	Merwin
Marita	Maynard	Meryl
Marj	Mead	Messie
Marja	Meara	Metta
Marjorie	Meg	Meyer
Marketa	Megan	Mia
Marleah	Meggie	Micah
Marleen	Meghan	Michael
Marlo	Mel	Michaelina
Marna	Mela	Michaeline
Marnie	Melanie	Michaella
Marquita	Melantha	Micki
Marrs	Melba	Midge
Marsh	Melina	Mignonette
Marsha	Melinda	Miguela
Marshell	Melisande	Miguelita
Mart	Melissa	Mike
Marta	Melita	Mikey
Marti	Mellicent	Mil
Mash	Mellie	Mildrid
Masha	Mello	Milena
Matilda	Melloney	Millisent
Matilde	Melody	Mindy
Matildette	Melum	Minna
Matrika	Melva	Minnie
Matt	Mendel	Minor
Mattie	Mendie	Mira
Maude	Mercedes	Mirabel
Maura	Mercy	Mirabella
Maureen	Meri	Mirabelle
Maurice	Meria	Mirella
Maurita	Meriel	Mirelle
Mavis	Merlina	Miriam
Maxi	Merline	Mirilla
Maxie	Merola	Mitch
Maxine	Merrielle	Mitchel

Mitri
Mitzi
Modesta
Modestia
Modestine
Mohammed
Moira
Molly
Mona
Monica
Monroe
Montgomery
Moore
Mopsey
Morena
Morene
Morgan
Morgano
Moria
Morie
Morris
Mort
Mortie
Mortimer
Moselle
Moses
Mozelle
Mr. Magoo
Muhammad
Muppet
Murdock
Muriel
Muriette
Murray
Murry
Myra
Myrna
Myron
Myrt

Myrta
Myrtice
Myrtie
Myrtle

—N—

Nadia
Nadine
Nady
Nan
Nana
Nance
Nancie
Nanette
Nanice
Nanine
Nannie
Naoma
Naomi
Nap
Napoleon
Nappie
Nat
Nata
Natala
Natalina
Nataline
Nate
Nathalie
Nathan
Natty
Neal
Ned
Neda
Neddie
Nedra
Neil
Nelda
Nelia

Nell
Nellie
Nells
Nellson
Nerissa
Nessie
Nestor
Nettie
Neville
Nevin
Nevins
Newt
Newton
Nibbles
Niccolo
Nick
Nickie
Nickolaus
Nicolette
Nicoli
Nicolina
Nicoline
Nicolos
Nigi
Nigil
Nika
Nike
Ninetta
Ninette
Ninon
Nip
Nipper
Nippie
Nissa
Nissie
Nita
Noah
Nobie
Noel

Noella
Noelle
Noellyn
Noelyn
Nola
Nolan
Nolana
Noland
Nora
Norah
Norbert
Norbie
Noreen
Norma
Norman
Normie
Norrie
Norris
Northrop
Norton
Nova
Novia
Nyd
Nydia
Nye
Nyssa

—O—

Oakes
Oakie Dokie
Oaks
Obadiah
Obed
Obediah
Obie
Octave
Octavia
Ode
Odel

Odelinda
Odella
Odetta
Odette
Odilia
Ogden
Olaf
Olga
Olin
Oliveette
Ollie
Olly
Olva
Olympe
Olympie
Omaha
Ona
Ondine
Onida
Oona
Opalina
Opaline
Oralie
Oren
Oriana
Oriane
Orion
Orland
Orlando
Orleans
Ormond
Orreo
Orrin
Orson
Orville
Osborn
Osgood
Osmond
Ossie

Oswald
Oswell
Otillie
Otis
Oxford
Ozzie

—P—

Pablo
Paddy
Paint
Palmer
Pam
Pamela
Pamelina
Pamella
Pammie
Pancho
Park
Parker
Parnell
Parrie
Pascal
Pasquale
Pat
Patches
Patrice
Patrizia
Patsy
Patton
Patty
Paula
Pauletta
Paulette
Paulina
Paulita
Pauly
Peaches
Pearla

Pearline
Pedro
Pee Wee
Peg
Pen
Penelopa
Penelope
Pepi
Pepper
Peppie
Percy
Perry
Pet
Peta
Peter
Petrina
Petronella
Petronia
Petula
Peyton
Phedra
Phelps
Phil
Phillie
Phillippine
Pierre
Pilar
Ping Pong
Pinky
Piper
Pippy
Pixie
Plato
Platon
Polly
Pollyanna
Pom
Pommeroy
Pommie

Porky
Porter
Portie
Prancer
Prentice
Prince
Princess
Princilla
Prissie
Private
Prudence
Prudi
Prue
Pryor
Puff
Pumpkin

—Q—
Quail
Quartz
Quasar
Quenie
Quenna
Quenton
Querida
Quiche
Quick Silver
Quinlon
Quinn
Quint
Quinta
Quintilla
Quintin
Quintinella
Quinton
Quintus
Quipper
Quiver

—R—
Rad
Radburn
Radcliff
Radie
Rae
Rafael
Rafe
Raff
Rafferty
Rainer
Raleigh
Ralph
Ram
Ramona
Ramsey
Rance
Rand
Randall
Ranee
Ranger
Ranson
Raoul
Raphael
Raquel
Rastus
Ray
Rayburn
Raynar
Raynor
Reba
Rebecca
Redford
Redneck
Reece
Reed
Reeve
Reggie
Reginald

Reid
Rem
Remington
Remus
Remy
Rena
Renata
Renate
Rene
Renie
Renold
Reuben
Reye
Reynard
Rhea
Rhett
Rhoda
Rhona
Rhonda
Rica
Ricca
Rich
Richard
Richie
Rickie
Rider
Riley
Ringo
Riordan
Rip
Roanna
Roanne
Robbie
Robena
Roberta
Roberto
Robin
Robinette
Robinson

Rochelle
Rochester
Rochette
Rock
Rockie
Rod
Roddie
Roderick
Rodger
Rodney
Rogerio
Rogers
Rollo
Rolly
Romain
Roman
Rona
Ronalda
Ronnie
Rory
Rosabel
Rosabella
Rosabelle
Rosalind
Rosalinda
Rosaline
Rosalyn
Rosamond
Rosanna
Rosanne
Rosia
Rosina
Rosita
Rossie
Rowena
Roxane
Roxanna
Roxanne
Roxie

Roxy
Roze
Rozele
Rozella
Rozita
Rubetta
Rubi
Rubia
Rubie
Rubina
Ruddy
Rudy
Rue
Rufe
Ruffle
Ruffles
Rummy
Rupert
Russ
Rusty
Ruth
Rutherford
Ruthan
Ruthie

—S—
Sabina
Sabrina
Sachiko
Sada
Sadelle
Sadie
Sal
Sallie
Saloma
Salomi
Salvador
Salvatore
Sam

Samara
Sammie
Sanborn
Sancho
Sandra
Sanford
Sapphire
Sara
Sasha
Sassy
Satin
Saul
Sawyer
Sax
Saxon
Saxton
Sayer
Scalawag
Scamp
Scott
Scotty
Scout
Scruff
Scruffy
Seamus
Sean
Sebastiano
Secretary
Selby
Seldon
Selena
Selinda
Selma
Serena
Serge
Seth
Seward
Sexton
Seymour

Shaina
Shamus
Shandy
Shane
Shani
Shannon
Shari
Sharon
Sheba
Sheehan
Sheena
Sheffie
Sheffield
Shelby
Sheldon
Shelly
Shelton
Shepherd
Sher
Sheridan
Sherlock
Sherwood
Sheryl
Shirleen
Shoshana
Sib
Sibbie
Sibel
Sibella
Sibelle
Sibley
Sid
Sidney
Siegfried
Sig
Sigmund
Silvan
Silvano
Silvester

Silvia
Silvie
Silvio
Simon
Simona
Simonette
Simonne
Sinclair
Sissie
Skelly
Skip
Skipper
Skippie
Sloan
Smitty
Sniffles
Snuffy
Sol
Soley
Sollie
Solomon
Somerset
Sondra
Sonia
Sonnie
Sonya
Sophie
Sophronia
Spark
Spec
Special
Spence
Spencer
Sphinx
Sprague
Spring
Sprite
Spumoni
Stacy

Stanford
Star
Steffie
Stepha
Stephana
Stephani
Stephen
Stephenus
Stephi
Stephie
Stevana
Steven
Stewart
Stillman
Storm
Stormie
Strike
Struffy
Strutter
Stu
Stuart
Stutter
Styles
Sue
Sukie
Sullivan
Sully
Summer
Sundance
Susan
Susana
Susanetta
Susanna
Susie
Sutherland
Sutton
Suzi
Sven
Svend

Sybil
Sydelle
Sydney
Sylvester
Sylvia

—T—
Tab
Tabbie
Tabitha
Tad
Tag
Talia
Tallie
Tallulah
Tamar
Tamara
Tamma
Tammi
Tang
Tangles
Tanner
Tanny
Tara
Tasha
Tate
Tav
Tavish
Taylor
Teague
Ted
Teddie
Teena
Telly
Tempest
Templeton
Terence
Teresa
Tess

Tessa
Tessie
Tex
Thaddaus
Thalassa
Thane
Thelma
Theo
Theobold
Theodore
Theresa
Thimble
Thomas
Thomasa
Thomasin
Thomasina
Thor
Thora
Thordia
Thordis
Thorndike
Thornie
Thornton
Thorpe
Thuston
Tiff
Tiffany
Tiffie
Tigger
Tilda
Tildie
Tim
Timmy
Timothea
Tina
Tine
Tinka
Tinker
Tinkerbelle

Tinsel
Tish
Tisha
Tita
Titania
Titus
Tobias
Todd
Toddie
Tommie
Toni
Tonia
Toots
Tore
Tory
Toto
Townie
Townsend
Trace
Tracie
Travis
Tray
Trent
Trev
Tricia
Tricks
Tricksie
Trina
Trinka
Tris
Trista
Tristan
Trix
Trixie
Troubles
Troy
Truda
Trudie
Truffles

Truly
Tuesday
Tuff Stuff
Tuffy
Tully
Twinkie
Twinkle
Twitter
Ty
Tynaner
Tyrus
Tyson

—U—
U
Udale
Udall
Udell
Ukelele
Ulriah
Ulric
Ulrica
Ultra
Umeko
Una
Uncle Whiskers
Unity
Uppity
Upton
Urchin
Uri
Uriah
Ursa
Ursala
Ursulina
Ursuline
Uta
Utopia

—V—
Val
Valaree
Valaria
Vale
Valeda
Valencia
Valentina
Valera
Valerie
Valida
Vallie
Van
Vance
Vanessa
Vania
Vanna
Vannie
Veda
Vel
Velma
Ven
Venie
Venita
Venus
Vera
Veradis
Vere
Verena
Verene
Veria
Verina
Vern
Verna
Vernie
Vernon
Veronica
Vic
Vick

Vickie	Wandie	Willabella
Vida	Wandis	Willamina
Vina	Ward	Willetta
Vince	Warden	Willette
Vinna	Waring	William
Vinnie	Warner	Willie
Viola	Warren	Wilma
Violanna	Washburn	Wilmette
Viole	Washout	Wilone
Virg	Washy	Wilt
Virgil	Waverly	Wilton
Virgilio	Waxahatchie	Winner
Virginia	Wayland	Winnie
Virgo	Wayne	Winnifred
Virtue	Webb	Winola
Vita	Weber	Winona
Viv	Webster	Winter
Vivian	Wells	Winthrop
Viviana	Wendell	Wit
Vivianne	Wendie	Witty
Vivie	Werner	Wolf
Vivien	Wes	Wolfgang
Vixen	Wesley	Wolfie
Von	Westbrook	Wolverine
Vonna	Weston	Wood
Vonnie	Wheeler	Woodie
	Whiskers	Woodrow
—W—	Whit	Woolite
Waite	Whitman	Worth
Wakefield	Whitney	Worthy
Wald	Whittaker	Wright
Waldemar	Whity	Wyatt
Walker	Wil	Wye
Wallace	Wilbert	Wylie
Wallie	Wilbur	Wynn
Wallis	Wiley	
Wally	Wilhelmina	**—X—**
Walton	Wilhelmine	Xantha
Wanda	Willa	Xanthus

Xaviera
Xena
Xeno
Xenophon
Xerox
Ximenes
X-tra

—Y—
Yahoo
Yance
Yankee
Yehundi
Yetta
Yipper
Yippy
Ynez
York
Yorkie
Yosh
Yoshi

Yoshiko
Yo Yo
Yucca
Yucky
Yule
Yummy
Yves
Yvette
Yvinne

—Z—
Zacarias
Zak
Zane
Zanie
Zany
Zarah
Zared
Zaria
Zeb
Zebulon

Zed
Zedekiah
Zeke
Zelda
Zena
Zenia
Zia
Ziggy
Zig Zag
Zilvia
Zipp
Zippora
Zita
Zitella
Zoe
Zola
Zollie
Zora
Zorana
Zorina
Zorine

AUTHORS' SKETCH

Wanda and Texe Marrs are great lovers of pets. Active in the Humane Society and other organizations devoted to the welfare of dogs, cats, and other animals, the Marrs are also owners of a detective agency which specializes in finding missing pets. Wanda manages this agency, one of only two in the United States, and Texe is a college professor.

Wanda and Texe are authors of four other non-fiction books and have been published in the *National Enquirer, Sunday Woman, VFW, Elks, Group, Friends,* and many other national magazines. The Marrs reside in Austin, Texas, with Minnie, a white poodle, and Muffin, a poodle/terrier mix.

*"Don't worry, Fluffy, Daddy will take care of that big bulldog
that's been picking on you."*

128